Praise for *Every Step Is Home*

"A beautiful successor to Steinbeck
Kerouac's *On the Road*, Lori Erickson
nates our spiritual connection to the r
of the heart' reminds us that our futu
connection."

　　　　　　　　　　—Richard Louv, author of *Our Wild Calling*
　　　　　　　　　　　　　　and *Last Child in the Woods*

"In this good-humored, rich blend of travelogue, spiritual reflection, and scientific inquiry, Lori Erickson asks and answers the question: If we engage deeply and intimately with nature's sacred places, will we ever go back inside for spiritual experience? Using the author's model of curiosity, wonder, and mindful attention, readers will be inspired to undergo their own spiritual quests to sacred sites near and far."
　　　　　　　　　　　　—Beth Norcross, Executive Director,
　　　　　　　　　　　　The Center for Spirituality in Nature

"As a fellow nomad, I resonate with the author's discovery of the sacred in surprising places across the United States. This travelogue will encourage you to stretch your own spirituality with an invitation to explore the natural world as a touchstone to the shared story of God's people."
　　　　　　—Stephanie Fritz, Coordinator for Christian Formation in the
　　　　　　Presbyterian Church (U.S.A.), full-time RVer, and digital nomad

"Movement and stillness, rhythm and silence, taking a trip and going home—this book will give you all that at once. Erikson creates a physical space with words. It's a place where you can breathe deeply—in spite of everything. We all need more places like that."
　　　　　　　—Erin Wathen, pastor and author, www.homeandholler.com

Praise for *The Soul of the Family Tree*

"*The Soul of the Family Tree* posits that a spiritual grounding in one's family history can combat 'historical amnesia' and nurture a sense of belonging."

　　　　　　　　　　　　　　　　　—*Foreword Reviews*

"Erickson discovers the well of wisdom by the roots of every family tree—those stories that influence our inner lives—and celebrates the explorer in all of us."
—Nancy Marie Brown, author of *The Far Traveler* and *The Real Valkyrie*

"This truly entertaining book should be on the shelf of everyone who is interested in family history, genealogy, or who has ever wondered, 'Where do I come from, really?'"
—June Melby, author *My Family and Other Hazards*

Praise for *Near the Exit*

"Open-hearted and soulful, never morbid, and often uplifting, *Near the Exit* is a colorful travelogue of mortality."
—Ira Byock, author of *Dying Well* and *The Best Care Possible*

"*Near the Exit* is a delicious, funny, and quite moving read. Part *actual* travelogue, it's also a *spiritual* exploration of death. . . . Highly recommend for people of any or no faith practice."
—Jennifer Grant, author of *Love You More* and *Maybe I Can Love My Neighbor Too*

"*Near the Exit* is an intriguing exploration of late life and death that will sometimes cause you to squirm or to laugh out loud. Always though, it will prompt you to think deeply about what it is to be mortal."
—Missy Buchanan, advocate, writer, and speaker for older adults

"You simply don't expect a book about loss and mortality to be the exceptional read that *Near the Exit* is. . . . Her prose is a rich teaching that seamlessly includes the rituals of many cultures, travel, and the beautiful intimacy of saying goodbye to someone you love."
—Paula D'Arcy, author of *Stars at Night*, *Winter of the Heart*, and *Gift of the Red Bird*

Every Step Is Home

Also by Lori Erickson

The Soul of the Family Tree: Ancestors, Stories,
and the Spirits We Inherit

Near the Exit: Travels with the Not-So-Grim Reaper

Holy Rover: Journeys in Search of Mystery, Miracles, and God

Every Step Is Home

A Spiritual Geography
from Appalachia to Alaska

Lori Erickson

WJK WESTMINSTER
JOHN KNOX PRESS
LOUISVILLE • KENTUCKY

© 2023 Lori Erickson

First Edition
Published by Westminster John Knox Press
Louisville, Kentucky

23 24 25 26 27 28 29 30 31 32—10 9 8 7 6 5 4 3 2 1

All rights reserved. No part of this book may be reproduced or transmitted in any form or by any means, electronic or mechanical, including photocopying, recording, or by any information storage or retrieval system, without permission in writing from the publisher. For information, address Westminster John Knox Press, 100 Witherspoon Street, Louisville, Kentucky 40202-1396. Or contact us online at www.wjkbooks.com.

Unless otherwise indicated, Scripture quotations are from the New Revised Standard Version, Updated Edition, copyright © 2021 National Council of Churches of Christ in the United States of America. Used by permission. All rights reserved worldwide.

An adapted version of chapter 1 was first published in *The Other Journal: An Intersection of Theology & Culture*, Issue 33: Reimagination, June 18, 2021.

A portion of the poem "Unmarked Boxes," in Jalal Al-Din Rumi, *The Essential Rumi*, translated by Coleman Barks, with John Moyne (New York: HarperCollins, 1995) is reprinted with the permission of translator Coleman Barks.

Photo for prologue courtesy of Iowa Tourism Office; photo for chapter 1 courtesy of Lori Erickson; photo for chapter 2 courtesy of Nebraska Tourism; photos for chapters 3, 5, 6, 7, 9, 10, and 11 courtesy of Bob Sessions; photo for chapter 4 courtesy of NPS/J. Borden; photo for chapter 8 courtesy of Travel South Dakota. All photos are used by permission.

Book design by Drew Stevens
Cover design by designpointinc.com
Cover art by Susan Trudinger. Used by permission.

Library of Congress Cataloging-in-Publication Data is on file at the Library of Congress, Washington, DC.

ISBN-13: 978-0-664-26832-9

PRINTED IN THE UNITED STATES OF AMERICA

♾ The paper used in this publication meets the minimum requirements of the American National Standard for Information Sciences—Permanence of Paper for Printed Library Materials, ANSI Z39.48-1992.

Most Westminster John Knox Press books are available at special quantity discounts when purchased in bulk by corporations, organizations, and special-interest groups. For more information, please e-mail SpecialSales@wjkbooks.com.

For Owen and Melissa

But do not ask me where I am going,
As I travel in this limitless world,
Where every step I take is my home.

—Eihei Dōgen

Contents

Effigy Mounds National Monument in Iowa preserves more than two hundred prehistoric Indigenous mounds, thirty-one of which are in the shape of bears or birds. (PHOTO CREDIT: IOWA TOURISM OFFICE)

Prologue
The Marching Bears of Iowa

Not far from where I grew up in northeastern Iowa, ten bears march across a high bluff overlooking the Mississippi River. They've been marching there for at least eight centuries, in rain and snow and sunshine, through seasons of drought and rain, silent witnesses to an ever-changing world around them. Unconcerned by the occasional airplane flying overhead and the barges passing by on the river below, the bears continue their steady, mysterious march.

As a travel writer who specializes in holy places, I'm embarrassed to say that for most of my life I've ignored this spiritual treasure in my own backyard. I visited Effigy Mounds National Monument mainly for hiking, largely oblivious to its more than two hundred prehistoric Indigenous mounds, thirty-one of which are in the shape of bears or birds. And I'd never even visited its most significant site—the Marching Bear Group that stretches for nearly a quarter mile across the top of a bluff.

In my defense, it's easy to overlook earthen mounds like these, which are among the many thousands built by the native peoples of North America before Europeans arrived on the continent. Through the past centuries the great majority have been plowed and bulldozed, and even those that remain require some effort and imagination to appreciate. Without a trained eye, a prehistoric mound, even a bear-shaped one, can look like just another small hill covered by grass.

But once I discovered those Marching Bears, once I'd walked and sat and prayed among them, I've come to realize that they carry a powerful spiritual message, one with multiple layers of meaning. In reflecting on them, I realize that this sacred site is from a culture that's not mine, and that I'm only a visitor there. But the sign at the entrance to the monument invites the public to experience Effigy Mounds as a sacred place, and I'm not one to refuse such an invitation.

One message from those bears is that the spiritual path calls for subtlety and discernment. Just as it's easy to overlook these mounds, it's easy to miss the sacred that threads through all of life. The Marching Bears appear quite different from overhead—the raptors that glide on the breezes above them, in other words, have the best view. So maybe the lesson here is that the sacred requires us to shift perspective, to get out of our ordinary plane of existence and find a new vantage point.

My time among the Marching Bears has made me want to explore other sacred landmarks in America, this country that's so new in some ways and so ancient in others. That's an important lesson for me, especially, because I've made a career out of writing about spiritual sites around the world. I've loved my trips to places as far away as Egypt, New Zealand, and Peru, but increasingly I want to see the sacred everywhere, not only in distant lands. Just as pilgrims walk the sacred paths abroad with reverence, I think we can find hallowed routes in the United States, and in doing so perhaps find points of connection in a society that can seem hopelessly fragmented.

The travels in this book reflect a restlessness in my own spiritual life, a condition that I've ruefully recognized is probably a perpetual state for me. While I don't want to leave organized Christianity behind, too often it feels like a room with its windows nailed shut. It isn't that I disagree with its doctrines or rituals: it's just that they feel stale. I want to get out and move, to explore, to feel the spirit moving through me in unexpected ways. That's why these sacred sites have been a beacon to me. Among them, I've eagerly sought out new vantage points, emulating those eagles soaring above the Marching Bears of Iowa.

Just after I began working on this book, the sudden, shocking spread of COVID-19 and the upheavals it brought to the world forced yet another vantage point on me. As many parts of the globe went into lockdown and fear and anxiety multiplied, one of my reactions was the entirely selfish thought of how I could possibly write a travel book during a time when I couldn't travel. (Yes, go ahead and cue the world's smallest violin. I realize that among those who deserve sympathy during a pandemic, travel writers rank near the bottom.) Even worse than not being able to research my book was that my soul was withering, and the longer I stayed home, the worse it got. As I grew ever more bored and dispirited while confined close to home, a new, deeper focus for this book came into being. I realized how much I was learning about traveling by *not* traveling, and how missing this much-loved part of my life made me appreciate as never before how wanderlust feeds my spirit.

I think my restlessness of soul has been shared by many people during the pandemic. Cut off from offices, churches, schools, restaurants, and other places where we normally interacted, millions of us have sought sustenance in nature. The outdoors has become a kind of *third place*, a term used to describe settings beyond the realms of home and work where people gather to play, socialize, and rejuvenate.

Even now that the pandemic has waned, I've found myself thinking more and more about how COVID-19 has changed our global spiritual landscape. Around the world, as more and more people are discovering the transformative power of nature, as campgrounds fill and parks overflow with visitors, there are changes percolating beneath the surface that I think will have profound effects on spirituality in the coming decades. What does it mean to seek the spirit outside the walls of a building, to study what the early Celtic Christians called the Book of Creation, which they believed was as full of divine revelation as the Bible? What makes a place holy? And once we find spiritual inspiration outside, will we ever want to go back inside to worship?

Effigy Mounds National Monument is a good place to think about these questions. From its visitor center, a hiking trail leads up a bluff to a plateau high above the Mississippi, where it winds beneath tall oaks, maples, hickory and other hardwood trees. The path leads to Fire Point, where you can see the river four hundred feet below, its braided channels flowing past forested islands. In the winter, bald eagles soar on the updrafts created by the bluff; in summer, the woods are alive with birdsong.

Signs along the hiking trail point out the mounds, which blend seamlessly into the natural landscape. While the native peoples of North America built mounds in many places, effigy mounds—which are in the shape of an animal—are much more unusual. In this part of northeastern Iowa and across the Mississippi River in southwestern Wisconsin, bear and bird effigies are the most common, but elsewhere in Wisconsin are mounds in the shape of creatures that include deer, bison, lynx, turtle, and panther.

Here at the monument, the largest earthen structure is the Great Bear Mound, a huge creature lying on its side. If this bear stood up it would be seventy feet in height—a formidable animal indeed to encounter on an afternoon walk. There are less showy mounds here too; some are circular, others are in the form of rounded rectangles, and a third type is a combination of the two, so that the mound looks a necklace of huge beads. The mounds rise to a height of two to eight feet above the forest floor, their shapes delineated by grass that's allowed to grow to a greater height than the surrounding turf.

All of these earthen works were created between 850 and 1,400 years ago by hunter-gatherers who lived off the rich resources of this fertile river valley. They harvested fish and mussels from the Mississippi, hunted deer and elk, and foraged for berries, wild rice, acorns, and other foods in the wetlands and forests of the region. In the midst of it all they found time to carry countless baskets of earth to form mounds, laboriously shaping some of them into animal forms.

Because these people left no written records, we can only guess why the mounds were built or how they were used. Many of the mounds contain human remains, but they likely had ceremonial uses as well. Perhaps mound-building marked celestial events or delineated boundaries between groups. Maybe it was a way to connect with ancestors, mark the arrival of a season, or affirm clan identities.

Sometime around 850 years ago the building stopped. The shift coincided with a change to a more settled agricultural existence, with people living in larger villages instead of small groups. Then in the late 1600s, European fur traders began arriving in the area, followed in the 1840s by an influx of settlers, who logged and plowed the land containing the mounds, oblivious to their significance. Surveys in the 1800s and early 1900s list more than ten thousand mounds in northeastern Iowa alone; within a century, fewer than a thousand were left. Thankfully, the ones at Effigy Mounds were preserved in a national monument in 1949.

President Harry Truman created the monument because of its archaeological significance, and throughout the 1950s and '60s, excavations were done on many of the mounds. In the 1970s Indigenous rights groups started speaking out against the practice of excavating native burials, which led to many changes in how archaeologists treat prehistoric sites. Especially after a criminal case in 2016 involving an Effigy Mounds superintendent who kept Indigenous remains in his own possession, today the U.S. National Park Service works hard to maintain good relations with twenty tribes affiliated with Effigy Mounds National Monument. Among them are the Ho-Chunk, Otoe-Missouria, Winnebago, Sac and Fox, Santee Sioux, and the Iowa Tribe of Kansas and Nebraska. Ceremonies are occasionally held there, and prayer bundles, ties, and flags can be seen throughout the park.

Having grown up less than an hour away from Effigy Mounds, I've visited the monument many times through the years, but it wasn't until I discovered the Marching Bear Group that I began to better understand why tribal nations value it so highly as a spiritual landmark. These mounds are located in a part of the park that gets less use than the trails near the visitor center. On top of a high bluff, a row of ten bear-shaped effigies runs through a corridor of green grass bordered by trees. Though the individual bears are about twenty feet shorter than the Great Bear Mound, if they got up and started marching past me the line would stretch beyond my line of sight, an ursine parade of massive power.

I have a lot of questions about these bears. What did they mean to the people who built them? What rituals were done here? Why are there so many bear effigies in one spot? Why are they all facing the same direction? I'll never know the answers to these questions, but on a summer day it's pleasant to speculate on them, giving me something to think about as I soak up the sun, the view, and the fresh air.

As I settle deeper into the silence, the quiet holiness of the site laps at the edges of my consciousness. I've been to sacred sites around the world, from ornate cathedrals and temples filled with devotees to sacred mountains with their tops wreathed in clouds. The sense of holiness at Effigy Mounds is subtler, perhaps more in keeping with midwestern sensibilities, but there's an undeniable sense of the sacred here, fully as palpable as at any of those other landmarks. I get the sense of being part of a long line of pilgrims who have traveled here for renewal and inspiration.

The fact that the Marching Bears appear to be walking is a spiritual lesson in itself. It makes me realize how sedentary much of contemporary religion is, even before COVID-19 sentenced many of us to the soul-sapping miseries of Zoom worship. With rituals that typically have us sitting quietly inside buildings, we seem to believe that God won't pay attention to us unless we act like well-behaved schoolchildren in a class led by a strict teacher.

This runs counter to the fact that humans are designed to *move*, both in our ordinary routines and in our spiritual lives. Millennia ago, our hominid ancestors began to walk upright, igniting an evolutionary transformation that's still being played out. Walking on two legs is more energy efficient than on four, allowing these early humans to cover greater distances. It helped them spot predators and prey, and it freed their hands to carry burdens and use tools. There are disadvantages to be sure, as anyone with a bad back realizes (since walking upright puts a lot of weight on our lower back and hips). But the benefits of walking far outweigh the disadvantages, and you can make a good argument that no other evolutionary change was more important in creating *Homo sapiens*.

We've evolved a long way from our hominid ancestors, but we continue to benefit from walking. It strengthens our heart and lungs, improves the functioning of our immune system, enhances digestion, strengthens bones, and pumps blood to our brain. The feel-good hormones released by it improve our psychological health, lightening mood and easing depression. A walk helps us step off the hamster wheel of anxiety, even for just a short time.

I think all those millennia of walking have shaped our souls too. A walk, especially in a beautiful natural setting, allows for open-ended thinking that doesn't happen as easily in the midst of regimented daily routines. As the scene before us slowly shifts, our eyes drift from one view to another, inviting contemplation and reflection. Walking isn't as conducive to linear thought—you're unlikely to be able to solve a complicated mathematical equation while strolling—but it lends itself instead to intuitions, flashes of insight, and making connections between seemingly disparate things. Walking, in other words, allows our consciousness to expand and deepen. Echoing the experiences of many, St. Augustine of Hippo put it this way: *Solvitur ambulando* ("It is solved by walking"). No matter what "it" is, it's usually made better by taking a walk.

Looking around the global religious landscape, it's clear that many faiths have a sense of the importance of walking as a spiritual practice. Buddhists do walking meditation, Muslims circumambulate the Kaaba in Mecca during the Hajj, and Hindus make a reverent clockwise circuit around sacred places as a form of prayer. "Walk as if you are kissing the Earth with your feet," said Buddhist teacher Thich Nhat Hanh.

In Christianity, the Bible is full of walkers, which isn't surprising given that it was written in a premodern age. But walking often has powerful symbolic meanings, including when the Israelites wandered for forty years in the desert or when Jesus went into the desert to pray (where he encountered the devil, which is a reminder that not all walks are harmless). Jesus often invited his followers to walk with him, and in his final hours he walked through the streets of Jerusalem on a path that came to be known as the Via Dolorosa, which pilgrims follow to this day. Another great walker was Paul, whose missionary journeys covered many thousands of miles. God himself promises to walk among his people, a promise that the psalmist recalls as he walks through the valley of the shadow of death. Christians are told to walk in the light, though when they're not welcomed in a particular area, they're told to shake the dust from their feet and keep on walking.

The practice of pilgrimage is another testimony to the transforming power of journeys on foot. Through the centuries the classic pilgrimages in many faiths have required weeks or months, and sometimes even years, of walking. These trips were often so dangerous that pilgrims would put all their affairs in order before they left, not knowing if they would return. And for Christians who couldn't make the long journey to Rome or Jerusalem, a labyrinth was constructed in Chartres Cathedral in France, whose twists and turns allowed people to make a symbolic walking pilgrimage.

The contemporary world is rediscovering the power of pilgrimage. Even in an age of high-speed travel in many forms, modern pilgrimages often involve considerable physical effort, which is actually essential because the journey is as important as the destination. Some walk the Camino de Santiago in Spain; others take a more secular version of a pilgrimage along the Appalachian or Pacific Crest Trail. The labyrinth has been rediscovered as well, with many retreat centers and churches installing one as a meditative tool.

All of these practices reinforce the timeless truth that in the steady rhythm of putting one foot in front of another, our souls slowly change. Perhaps it's because at some deep level we feel the pull of gravity with each step and know that we will one day return to the earth beneath our feet. Or maybe in walking we connect to a circuit of energy that allows the holiness of creation to flow more easily through us.

In this book I describe landscapes and experiences scattered across the United States from Appalachia to Alaska, most outside and many best experienced by walking. Some are clearly sacred in origin, while others require us to look more deeply beneath their surface to see the holiness. In each of these sites I reflect as well on a seemingly ordinary element such as air, fire, water, and stone that becomes sacred within the context of that place. Even if you can't travel to these destinations, I hope my reflections will prompt you to be more attuned to the sacredness of your own daily routines and your own neighborhood.

In these pages I invite you to travel with me to El Santuario de Chimayó in New Mexico, where pilgrims gather dirt that's said to have healing properties, and to Nebraska to see one of the world's most spectacular bird migrations. In Ohio I discover a huge serpent that's been coiling its way down a bluff for many centuries, and in Minnesota I explore a place where sacred stone is quarried. I wander through a cathedral of forest giants in California, soak in holy springs in Oregon, penetrate deep into a sacred cave in Tennessee, and learn about sacred animals from South Dakota bison. After marveling at Alaska's northern lights and Hawai'i's volcanoes, I end my journey in New Mexico's Chaco Canyon, where I ponder the intertwining of earth and heaven in sacred astronomy.

Through all my explorations, I've returned regularly to Effigy Mounds. On one of my visits, I wasn't surprised to learn that when park officials invited native elders to perform a ceremony at the park after a hiatus of many years, the religious leaders chose to conduct their first ceremony at the Marching Bears. Something about them is sacred, as anyone who spends time among them with an open heart will realize.

As for me, during the time I've researched and traveled and written about the holy sites in this book, I've felt those bears walking with me, reminding me to look beneath the surface to see the extraordinary hidden in the ordinary.

People come to El Santuario de Chimayó in New Mexico for dirt that's said to have healing properties. (Photo credit: Lori Erickson)

1

Dirt: El Santuario de Chimayó in New Mexico

Few substances are as maligned as dirt. If we're dirt poor, our only option is to get things dirt cheap. We can treat someone like dirt, which may include digging up dirt on them. We take off our shoes so we don't drag dirt into the house, we let dirty dishes soak in the sink, and we throw dirty clothes in the washer. Just don't air your dirty laundry in public—that's a big no-no.

But in Chimayó, New Mexico, the dirt is holy—and as I began a quest to find the sacred in America, that's the place that drew me first. If even dirt can be considered holy, surely anything can.

There was another reason why I wanted to visit the healing shrine of Chimayó: my mother's death at the age of ninety after several years in a memory-care unit in a nursing home. A month after that loss, the thought of visiting this pilgrimage site, famed for its sacred soil, came out of nowhere and wouldn't let me go. Perhaps it was tied to the fact that my mom had been an Iowa farmer's wife with deep roots in the earth, and so, in the paradoxical logic of the spiritual realm, Chimayó would be the perfect place to say goodbye to her. Or maybe it was simply that I needed healing, now that I was an orphan—a middle-aged one, to be sure, but an orphan nevertheless.

The weekend before I flew to New Mexico, a funeral director handed me a box that contained my mother's earthly remains. "Here's Mom," he said with incongruous good cheer.

I took the box, gingerly, and wondered what I would do with it until we held her service in the spring. The mantelpiece in my living room? It didn't seem right to display it in public. Storing it in the basement felt disrespectful, and I definitely didn't want it in my bedroom. So finally I settled on my office, a little upstairs room that once was a walk-in closet. I put the box of cremains next to a statue of the Virgin Mary, then draped a scarf over both Mary and the box so it looked like it was tucked under her arm. I would glance at it occasionally as I worked, wondering when I'd have the courage to open its lid and look inside.

As I was packing for my trip, I briefly considered taking some ashes with me to Chimayó, following the example of friends who'd scattered the remains of loved ones in beautiful sites around the world. But my mother had disliked traveling when she was alive, and I guessed that her thoughts on the matter probably hadn't changed after her death.

Chimayó, which is sometimes called the Lourdes of America, has long been on my radar as one of the most significant holy sites in the United States. My first two visits were separated by ten years, and during that time the shrine had grown in popularity, with the addition of a visitor center and outdoor spaces where groups can have services. I was a little hesitant to return for a third time, hoping that it hadn't become too commercialized or gentrified—but then I remembered that the whole shrine was centered on dirt, which would make it hard for it to get too uppity.

Long before the Spaniards arrived in the region, Chimayó was considered holy by the Pueblo people, who believed that healing spirits inhabited the hot springs in the area. After the springs dried up, people came for the dirt where the water had once been. The miracles, apparently, didn't mind whether they came through water or soil.

Chimayó's fame spread to the larger world around the year 1810, when a story began to circulate of a local man, Bernardo Abeyta, who saw a light springing from one of the hills near the Santa Cruz River. After following the light to its source, he found in the earth a crucifix bearing a dark-skinned Jesus. The local villagers paid homage to the relic and then took it to a church in nearby Santa Cruz. Myste-riously, during the night the crucifix returned to its origi-nal location. After this happened two more times, the locals received permission to build a small chapel to house the cru-cifix in Chimayó.

Our Lord of Esquipulas, as the figure on the crucifix is known, is also linked to a shrine in Guatemala associated with healing earth. Franciscan friars helped spread devotion to this icon throughout Mexico and New Mexico. It must have seemed natural to them to link the Pueblo people's stories about the site's healing earth to the Catholic devotion to Our Lord of Esquipulas.

And so through the years, the story of the crucifix became intertwined with earlier Indigenous beliefs, a story repeated countless times through history. The stones from pagan tem-ples get reused for churches; cathedrals are built over earlier sacred sites; churches whose congregations have dwindled become houses of worship for other faiths. The Holy Spirit seems to love recycling as much as environmentalists.

Humble Chimayó's reputation for miracles gradually spread, drawing an increasing number of pilgrims to the simple adobe church whose official name is El Santuario de Chimayó. After World War II, survivors of the Bataan Death March made a walking pilgrimage to the church on Good Friday in gratitude for their deliverance. The tradition of Holy Week pilgrimages continues to this day, when more than thirty thousand people walk to the church before Easter. Many travel the eight miles from the town of Nambé, while others walk from as far away as Santa Fe or Albuquerque.

My own pilgrimage began with a flight to Albuquerque in February, followed by a two-hour drive north, first on a broad highway and then on narrower roads that led me into dry, brown hills covered with sparse grasses and scattered junipers. At last I reached Chimayó, a village of about three thousand in the foothills of the Sangre de Cristo Mountains. When I pulled into the parking lot at the shrine there were just a couple of other cars there, a consequence of visiting in the low season of February. The wind was chilly as I walked past deserted outdoor shrines to the Virgin Mary and alcoves holding statues of saints. It all looked a little forlorn, like a party room after the celebration is over.

But once I entered the church, I found it as warm and inviting as I remembered from my previous two visits. The adobe church with twin bell towers is one of the finest examples of Spanish Colonial architecture in New Mexico, with a timbered ceiling, rough-plastered interior walls, and simple wooden pews. Five *reredos* (panels of sacred paintings) done in colorful folk-art style adorn its walls, one behind the altar and two on each side of the nave. Above the altar hangs a six-foot crucifix, said to be the same one found by Bernardo Abeyta.

On my previous visit I'd attended a mass during which a priest gave a wonderful homily, full of good humor and kindness, to a church in which every pew was filled. Many of the people had seemed like locals, but I also heard Japanese and French conversations on my way out of the sanctuary. Today, in contrast, the church was empty except for me, though a stand with flickering candles near the altar showed that other pilgrims had been there before me that day.

I sat for some time in the simple sanctuary, grateful to be at my destination and pondering what had drawn me here. I wasn't seeking a miracle, unlike many who come here. My mother had lived a good and long life, and amid my sadness at her death I felt relief that her twilight journey through dementia was over. But I also sensed a fissure inside me, a recognition that some primal link had been broken. I was trying to find my bearings as I learned to live the rest of my life without either

parent. My eye was caught by a wooden bust of the Virgin
Mary looking down from a windowsill, and I felt grateful to
have her maternal gaze rest on me.

I stood up, walked past the altar, and exited the church to
the adjoining small room known as *El Pocito*, which in Spanish
means "little well." By tradition, this is the spot where Abeyta
found the crucifix in 1810. Bowing my head at the low entryway, I saw the small hole in the ground that I remembered
from my previous visits. About a foot in diameter, it's filled
with fine-grained dirt. This is the spot where thousands have
knelt, ladling handfuls of powdery soil into containers they
brought from home. I crouched down to pick up my own
handful of dust, feeling its coolness sift through my fingers,
thinking about the fact that I'd been to many shrines with holy
water, but never one with holy dirt.

Holy places where miracles are said to occur are pretty
common in the religious world, from the Christian shrines of
Lourdes in France and the Basilica of Our Lady of Guadalupe
in Mexico to sacred sites in many other faiths. I've visited such
places across the globe with great interest, curious about what
draws people to them. I remain an agnostic on the claims of
inexplicable physical cures, but I have no trouble believing that
genuine healing does happen at such shrines, though it most
commonly takes the form of a mending of hearts rather than a
dramatic cure.

Even at Chimayó, a certain matter-of-factness reigns. In a
2008 interview, Father Casimiro Roca, who served as rector
at the church for more than five decades, said that the dirt
is replenished each day by human hands, not miraculously
replenished as some believed. "I always tell people that I have
no faith in the dirt, I have faith in the Lord," he told a *New
York Times* reporter. "But people can believe what they want."

The room adjacent to El Pocito gave ample evidence of
the piety of those who come here seeking healing. A row of
crutches hung on one wall, presumably left by those who no
longer needed them, and photographs lined the walls testify-
ing mutely to the prayers that have been said here. I stood for

a long time looking at the faces of those in the photos: soldiers in uniform, elderly women in hospital beds, fresh-faced school children, tattooed motorcycle riders, babies with oxygen tubes. I spotted one that looked like my mom, an elderly woman with a kind smile. Blinking back tears, I pulled my jacket closer in the chilly room and then left the church.

THE BEAUTY OF BONES

Georgia O'Keeffe went searching for flowers, but instead she found bones.

The famed artist was on my mind as I set out from Chimayó for an afternoon of exploring. Her iconic images of whitened animal skulls, multicolored cliffs and canyons, and high desert vistas are indelibly linked to the region surrounding Ghost Ranch, which lies an hour north of Chimayó. I was longing to see for myself those stark panoramas so different from the tidy farms and hills of my native Iowa, wanting an outer landscape that matched my inner mood.

O'Keeffe became fascinated by New Mexico on a visit to Santa Fe in 1917 when she was twenty-nine years old. "From then on, I was always on my way back," she later said. For a number of years that meant summer visits from her home in New York, but in 1949 she moved permanently to the region, first to a house at Ghost Ranch and later to one in the small village of Abiquiú.

For years O'Keeffe's life was overshadowed professionally and personally by her husband, the photographer Alfred Stieglitz. In 1933 she experienced a crisis caused by his infidelities, though the two remained married until his death in 1946. Their marital difficulties accelerated her need to redefine herself in the starkness of the New Mexico desert. There she found new directions in her art and an inner strength that sustained her for a future that would be largely solitary. Keenly attuned to the power of nature, she sought out the strangeness hidden in the familiar, removing what was nonessential by emphasizing color and shape. The dramatic countryside of northern New Mexico, a landscape stripped down to its barest essentials, became her artistic and spiritual home.

Before O'Keeffe fell under the spell of New Mexico, many of her paintings had featured lush flowers. But because blooms are sorely lacking in the high desert, here she turned instead to collecting and painting bones from animals whose carcasses had been picked clean by scavengers and then bleached by the sun. "To me, [bones] are as beautiful as anything I know," she said. "To me they are strangely more living than the animals walking around. . . . The bones seem to cut sharply to the center of something that is keenly alive on the desert even though it is vast and empty and untouchable."

O'Keeffe loved the angles and shapes of the bones and was fascinated by the ways they could be used to frame and dramatize the landscape. Some of her best-known paintings show skulls she'd collected on her walks through the desert. We may see these works as meditations on mortality, but for her the skeletons were more a symbol of endurance and strength than of death. While bones eventually decompose into soil, in the desert they can last for many decades. And just as bones show the underlying structure of an animal—the reality hidden underneath its surface—O'Keeffe's paintings hint of deeper meanings hidden within the New Mexico landscape.

As I drove past the red cliffs and canyons near Ghost Ranch, I saw many scenes that were familiar to me from O'Keeffe's work. The mountain known as Pedernal loomed in the distance, a peak sacred to the Navajo and Jicarilla people and one that O'Keeffe painted many times. She said she thought that if she painted it often enough, God would give it to her, though in the end the opposite became true. After her death her ashes— which were actually pulverized bones, like all cremains—were scattered there, so that she became part of the mountain.

I could see why O'Keeffe felt so at home in this wild and open countryside, a landscape perfectly suited to her need for solitude. I felt my own deep craving to be alone here. Normally I seek out conversations with people on my trips, eager to learn about the place from their perspectives. On this journey my impulse was just the opposite. As O'Keeffe had realized before me, this is a good place to be alone.

I remembered touring O'Keeffe's home and studio in the small village of Abiquiú on my previous visit. She'd purchased a rundown house there in 1945, and after restoring it, she made it her home for all but the last two years of her life. On my tour, I was amused by the docent's reverent attitude toward the artist and her military-style enforcement of security measures, including forcing us to relinquish all the pens and pencils we had in our bags, as if we were likely to start drawing on the walls like kindergarteners. But as I listened to the story of O'Keeffe's life there and her almost-religious devotion to her art, I could see why she has become a kind of secular saint in this part of the world. Like the desert hermits of the third century in Egypt, she was often cantankerous and odd, which I guess are good traits to have if you're seeking meaning in a desert.

I pulled into the long drive leading to Ghost Ranch, which is now a spiritual retreat center that attracts visitors from around the world. A cold wind had sprung up, and a light dusting of snow covered the landscape of red, yellow, and gray badlands. I walked the paths between its rustic wooden buildings, thinking of the many pilgrims who find their way here each year. (Chimayó isn't the only magnet for spiritual seekers in this region.) While the house where O'Keeffe lived isn't open to the public, simply soaking up the atmosphere and scenery made me feel connected to her.

As I meandered, I thought of one of my favorite O'Keeffe paintings. *From the Faraway, Nearby* shows an antlered skull floating in the sky above a desert landscape. At first it looks like an ordinary skull, but then you realize it has a mythic quality, with far too many points on its antlers for any real animal. I love the painting's juxtaposition of the familiar and the dreamlike, the near and the distant. Its mood evokes something relating to what I was searching for: a deeper perspective on life, one that's comfortable with paradox and is rooted in a sacred landscape that only appears ordinary at first glance.

On the drive back to Chimayó I could see Pedernal in the distance, and I thought about O'Keeffe's ashes, gradually being incorporated into the mountain she loved, and my mom's ashes, tucked beneath Mary's arm in my office.

THE TREASURE BENEATH OUR FEET

Amid the array of ordinary substances made sacred in Christian rituals, dirt takes a back seat to bread, wine, and water. The major exception is Ash Wednesday, when many denominations hold services that include the imposition of ashes, which is a fancy way of saying they smear dirt on people's foreheads. Traditionally the black soot is created by burning the leftover palms from the previous year's Palm Sunday service, a reminder of the cyclic nature of all life. The shouts of praise and hosanna inevitably fade; the green branches become brittle. And on Ash Wednesday, they're pressed into service again to remind us that we're going to die. Too often in the religious world we sugarcoat reality, but not on this day. From dust we came, and to dust we will return.

But my time in Chimayó made me realize that the Christian understanding of dirt is more multifaceted than that. Sure, there are plenty of Bible verses that speak negatively of dirt, and I've known more than a few altar guild members with an evangelical zeal for removing it. But Christianity actually has a pretty good relationship with dirt, starting with the fact that in Genesis God creates the first humans from it (a creation story whose broad outlines are echoed in many traditions across the globe). The word *humus*, a synonym for soil, shares the same Latin root as *human* and *humanity*. These words are also related to *humility*, which is just what you're supposed to feel when the smudge of ashes on your forehead disintegrates into tiny black speckles on your nose, cheeks, and chin.

In the Gospels, a story that makes neat freaks uncomfortable is when Jesus spits into the dust, forms a paste, and puts it on the eyes of a blind man. Go wash it off, he tells him, and when the man obeys his eyesight is restored. Whatever Jesus was up to—and despite his divinity, he should never be put in charge of sterilization protocols in a hospital—it's obvious that he wasn't afraid of a little dirt. For most of human history that was a nearly universal characteristic.

One example of someone who loved working in the dirt is St. Phocas, the patron saint of gardeners. During the third century when the Roman Empire was persecuting Christians, this kindly man grew food for the poor. One day a group of soldiers knocked on his door, asking for directions to the house of a Christian named Phocas, whom they were to arrest and execute. He cordially invited them in, offered them food, and put them up overnight. In between his hospitality duties he went out into his garden and dug a man-size hole in its rich loam. The next morning he told the soldiers that he was the person they were looking for, then asked them if they would be so kind as to kill him next to the grave he'd dug, so that his body could fertilize the garden.

The story of Phocas underscores the fact that death is intricately tied to soil, which is the greatest recycler on earth. Without its regenerative power, the corpses of once-living things would overwhelm us. Instead, the soil's microbes, fungi, and invertebrates take what is given to them and return the nutrients and carbon back into forms that can be used again. Thus, all of us are recycled plant and animal material, the culmination of many trillions of lives, large and small.

To learn more about what science can tell us about dirt, I turned to my friend Art Bettis, a geologist who specializes in soil. The first thing he did was set me straight on terminology. "Dirt is the stuff you get on your shoes," he said. "Soil is a living substance that sustains all terrestrial life. It's the most valuable—and the most unknown—ecosystem that we have.

And it's full of information about the past, both the recent past and the distant past."

My crash course in soil science from Art gave me a much greater respect for the element I'd formerly ignored. The thin layer of soil on the outside of the earth—just 7 percent of the surface of the planet—was formed over millions of years from the weathering of rocks into mineral particles that gradually became mixed with organic matter, air, water, and living organisms. In wet tropical climates, it takes about two hundred years to form one centimeter of soil; in milder climates it can take twice as long—and to create truly rich, fertile soil takes several thousand years.

Once it's formed, that fertile topsoil is a miraculous wellspring of life. In addition to growing plants, it acts as a kind of lung, releasing and absorbing water vapor, carbon dioxide, and other gases. Billions of species dwell within soil, from molds and fungi to bacteria; in fact, just a single handful of soil contains more organisms than the entire human population of the earth.

Art opened my eyes as well to the tremendous diversity of soils across the globe. Scientists divide them into twelve orders, though those classifications are in a continual state of flux as research reveals more information. I was pleased to learn that states have official soils, just as they do state birds. Connecticut has the regal Windsor; North Carolina, the bow-tied Cecil; and Minnesota, the next-door-neighbor Lester. Less amusing, but more authentic to the Indigenous origins of the regions, are Idaho's Threebear and Rhode Island's Narragansett.

I don't mean to brag, but my own state of Iowa's official soil, Tama Silt Loam, is some of the best in the world, at least if you're trying to grow things. It has an intense, dark color and is teeming with nutrients, microbes, and animals from earthworms to mites. And according to Art, it didn't even exist eleven thousand years ago. "Tama Silt Loam began its evolution as a thin soil in Iowa's late glacial evergreen forest, then became thicker, but still organic poor as the vegetation shifted to deciduous forest," he said. "During the past six thousand years it became much richer after all the organic material of the tallgrass prairie ecosystem became incorporated into it. When it was first plowed, the prairie's topsoil was more than three feet deep in Iowa."

Art's words emphasize the dynamic nature of soil. Its composition changes depending upon factors such as rainfall quantity, what's decaying on top of it, and what's living in it. Despite being a substance with no legs or wings, it also has a surprising ability to move. It's estimated that twelve million tons of dust from the Sahara drop onto the Amazonian rainforest each year, for example, where its minerals help replenish rainwater-depleted soils. Other soil movement is much more negative, including the many tons of fertile topsoil that get washed away every year in the Midwest. While the thick roots of prairie plants once held midwestern soil in place, modern farming practices too often lead to significant erosion; as a result, that thick layer of topsoil that existed when the pioneers first came to the Midwest has been reduced by more than half. Given how long it takes to regenerate soil, that's an unsustainable phenomenon.

Of course, agriculture is just one of the ways in which soil benefits humans. Many of our most important medicines come from the soil, including more than five hundred types of antibiotics. Conversely, health researchers speculate that our rising rates of allergies and asthma may be linked to too much cleanliness. One piece of evidence is that children raised on farms have lower rates of these medical issues. As a farmer's daughter who ate more than her fair share of dirt while growing up, I suspect that my immune system benefited from the many workouts I gave it.

Although I appreciated my crash course in soil science from Art, I don't want to give up on that homely word *dirt*. Like many short, English words that derive from Old Norse, from *sky* and *lake* to *bug*, it retains a Viking earthiness—in fact, its original form of *drit* means "excrement." Because manure makes great fertilizer, that's not necessarily an insult. For thousands of years the main fertilizer on farms was manure, which adds nitrogen, phosphorus, and potassium to the soil. It was so valuable that in Europe young women's dowries were sometimes calculated according to how much manure was produced on their childhood farms.

What would it mean if we viewed dirt not only as valuable but also as holy, and not just at Chimayó but everywhere? If we did so, we'd be much less likely to let it wash off our fields and into rivers, like foolish spendthrifts who throw their money away without a care. Instead we'd be like St. Phocas, deeply conscious of our need to nourish and protect it. I think of the people of Effigy Mounds carrying countless baskets of earth to form ceremonial mounds. I suspect they had a sense of the preciousness of what they were carrying.

All of this reminds me of a joke. A group of scientists form a delegation to meet with God to give him his marching orders. There's no need for a divine being anymore, they claim, given all we know about science. "We can clone animals and manipulate genes to create living creatures faster and better than you can," they say. So God challenges them to a human-making contest, which they eagerly accept. After he invites them to go first, one of the scientists reaches down to scoop up a handful of dirt, until God interrupts him.

"Oh, no," God says. "You have to use your own dirt."

HEALING EARTH

I spent three days hanging around Chimayó, walking its meditation path near the Santa Cruz River, browsing the weaving shops for which the area is famous, and sitting quietly in the adobe church. Although about three hundred thousand people visit the area each year, my arrival in February meant that I had it largely to myself most of the time. Occasionally others would wander through, older people mostly, usually spending just a few minutes in the church before heading to El Pocito, the room with the holy dirt. I watched the other visitors, trying to guess what they were praying for. Recovery from illness, a pregnancy for a daughter, healing of a troubled marriage, comfort after receiving a terminal diagnosis? The flickering votive candles lit by pilgrims bore witness to their silent prayers.

I could see, too, the ways in which the shrine has ties to a variety of spiritual traditions. In its outdoor meditation gardens, for example, there's a statue dedicated to Our Lady of La Vang, which draws pilgrims of Vietnamese and Filipino descent. Her story dates back to 1798, when a group of Catholics who were fleeing religious persecution hid in the forest of La Vang in Vietnam. While praying the Rosary under a banyan tree, they saw a beautiful lady with an infant in her arms. She spoke words of comfort to them, promised to be with them, and directed them to gather leaves from nearby bushes to make a drink that would heal their illnesses. Mary appeared in the forest a number of times after this initial apparition, and La Vang became a famous holy site. I loved seeing her serene statue at Chimayó, her features reflective of her origin in Asia, a reminder of the many ways in which the holy is expressed here.

Nearby is a small chapel that reflects the Indigenous roots of the shrine. The word *Chimayó* comes from *Tsi-Mayoh*, which in the Tewa language refers to one of the four sacred hills that overlook the valley. The chapel's iconography incorporates Native American images and symbols, from the altar's candleholders shaped like ears of corn to a tableau of the Last Supper featuring people in the dress of various tribes.

I found it curious that the native traditions surrounding healing earth remain so strong here. I remembered Art telling me about the widespread practice of eating dirt in traditional cultures around the world, especially in areas where the soil provides essential minerals lacking in people's diets. In past centuries pilgrims ate the holy dirt here, too, though that practice has fallen out of favor. Instead, pilgrims are advised by the clergy to pray, confess their sins, and ask God for guidance and healing. If they like, they can then rub the blessed dirt over the parts of their bodies in need of healing, which actually isn't much weirder than a lot of medical folklore and would certainly help stimulate the placebo response, if nothing else. At some deep level we seem to know that the earth has healing powers, if we just pay attention to each step we take.

A block away from the shrine, I found another church that draws nearly as many visitors as the Santuario: the Chapel of the Holy Child of Atocha, whose devotion has roots in a story from Spain. In the thirteenth century, some Christians were being held captive in the Madrid neighborhood of Atocha. Their captors wouldn't allow any adults to bring them food or water—just children, whom they didn't see as a threat. That meant that those who had no family were suffering greatly. One day a young boy showed up with a basket of food and gourd of water for the prisoners. The soldiers let him through, and the next day he returned again, and then again and again. His basket and gourd miraculously remained full, despite the many men who ate and drank from them. The prisoners took this as an answer to their prayers, believing that the child was Jesus. The Holy Child of Atocha, as he was known, became a figure of devotion throughout Spain and later in Mexico.

In 1857 a resident of the Chimayó region, Severiano Medina, made a vow that if he recovered from an illness, he would make a pilgrimage of more than a thousand miles to a shrine in Zacatecas, Mexico, that is dedicated to the Holy Child of Atocha. After recovering and making the trek there and back, he built a chapel dedicated to this manifestation of the divine.

At the chapel I learned why survivors of the Bataan Death March started making pilgrimages to Chimayó. After the bombing of Pearl Harbor, nearly two thousand members of the New Mexico National Guard fought valiantly with Filipino soldiers against the Japanese invasion of the Philippines. Defeated after seven months of battle, the soldiers were forced to walk sixty-five miles to POW camps, a brutal march during which many died of exhaustion, dehydration, starvation, and violence. Of the seventy-five thousand U.S. and Filipino troops who began the march, an estimated ten thousand died along the way. The survivors spent forty months in a variety of POW prisons and slave labor camps, enduring harsh conditions that led to many more deaths. By the end of the war, only about half of the members of the New Mexico National Guard were still alive. Many attributed their survival to the Holy Child of Atocha, whom they believed watched over them in their time of greatest need.

Sitting in the church dedicated to the Holy Child, I realized it would be easy to misinterpret its iconography, which in contrast to the more somber, rough-hewn mood of the Santuario is much brighter and more modern, with an emphasis on the innocent Holy Child rather than the suffering Christ. But learning the story behind the Good Friday pilgrimage made me realize how the two churches are linked. Darkness and light, illness and healing, suffering and redemption are intertwined in both.

The World War II story also gave me new insights into the small statue of the Holy Child of Atocha that rests in a glass case behind the church's altar. The young boy is sleeping, his head propped up against his hand. The faithful believe he's dozing because each night he walks out from the church in search of those in need. Many pilgrims to this church leave small shoes as a gift, because the Holy Child wears them out so quickly in his travels.

It's not just pilgrims who walk in search of God, I realized as I sat in that quiet church. God walks in search of us as well.

A few weeks after returning from Chimayó, I attended an Ash Wednesday service at my Episcopal church. As a priest put a smudge of ash on my forehead, she repeated the familiar words, "From dust you came, and to dust you will return." I thought of my time in Chimayó, of the faithful who come day after day seeking the healing earth, a substance that just like the ash on my forehead was formed from the remains of countless living creatures and from elements sourced from distant stars.

I walked back to my seat, sanctified by holy dirt, making my own pilgrimage of the heart.

Each spring, more than 600,000 sandhill cranes gather along the Platte River in Nebraska in one of North America's most spectacular wildlife displays. (PHOTO CREDIT: NEBRASKA TOURISM)

2

Air: The Sandhill Crane Migration in Nebraska

My time in Chimayó convinced me that I wasn't entirely foolish to want to explore sacred elements and experiences in America. Excited by the possibilities of where to go next, I didn't pay much attention to the initial reports of a new virus that was spreading in China, though they did make me think of a conversation I'd had with a fellow guest in the Airbnb I'd rented in Santa Fe. Over coffee one morning he told me that he'd done consulting work for nonprofit health organizations around the world, including during the Ebola virus outbreaks in West Africa. Impressed by his credentials, I asked what he thought about the virus that was just gaining some attention on the world stage.

He shrugged. "It could be bad, or not so bad. It's too soon to tell."

"Well, at least it sounds like it's an easier disease to deal with than Ebola," I said.

"I hope so," he replied. "I very much hope so."

The increasingly serious news reports validated his concern. Was it safe to travel? Ever the optimist, I figured it was, especially because our next trip was to a place with few people, though the nonhuman population was large indeed: Nebraska, where I hoped more than a half-million birds could teach me about sacred air.

Planning a trip to explore the element of air had stumped me for a considerable time. None of the possibilities I thought of seemed quite right. Skydiving and parasailing weren't an option, given my fear of heights. Storm chasing sounded exciting but potentially dangerous, as well as tedious while you waited around for tornadoes to form. A friend gave me an alternative idea.

"When I think of sacred air, I think of birds," she said. "You should go see the sandhill crane migration. That's a spiritual experience if there ever was one."

Her suggestion felt right. I knew that the annual event ranks among the world's greatest wildlife migrations, an American version of the huge herds of animals on the African Serengeti. From late February through March, more than 600,000 sandhill cranes pass through central Nebraska on an epic journey that takes them from their wintering grounds in the southern United States and northern Mexico to breeding grounds in Alaska and Canada. Their job in Nebraska is to rest for a few weeks and gain weight, which they do by feeding in the fields and marshes that border the Platte River. At night they return to the braided sandbars of the shallow waterway, where they crowd together in raucous rookeries containing thousands of birds.

So one day in early March, Bob and I headed out of town to experience sacred air, courtesy of those birds in Nebraska. As we drove, we periodically tuned in to the news, though for the moment COVID-19 was more an intellectual curiosity than a reality.

We arrived in Kearney, a city of about 34,000 in central Nebraska, in the late afternoon. The weather was gray and wintry, and as I stepped out of the car in front of the town's tourism office, the wind sliced through my jacket. Shivering, I pulled it closer and hurried inside.

"You're here to see the cranes?" asked a smiling woman behind the counter. "You've come at a good time. We're close to the height of the migration."

Pulling out some brochures from below the counter, she gave me a quick overview of the area's crane-related sites, which include the Crane Trust Nature and Visitor Center and the Iain Nicolson Audubon Center at Rowe Sanctuary. Both offer guided viewing experiences, she explained, including over-nighting in a blind near the river, but we could also observe the birds on our own. On a map she pointed out public viewing places along the river.

"The best time for seeing the cranes is at dawn and dusk, but during the day you can drive around and watch them feed-ing in the fields," she said. "Just don't try to approach them, and don't trespass on private land. You can use your car as a blind as long as it's not on major paved roads."

As I left the office, she added, "And keep your eye out for migrating geese and ducks too—we've got a lot of them."

Nebraska in the early spring, it seems, is the place to be if you're a bird.

After settling into our hotel, Bob and I headed out for our first encounter with the cranes. Using the map from the visitor center, we drove south for a couple of miles to the Fort Kear-ney State Recreation Area. After parking our car, we walked for ten minutes to a footbridge that stretched across the river. About thirty people were there, all bundled against the cold, many carrying binoculars and cameras.

And then we waited, because birds don't follow a strict schedule. I passed the time by doing some human watching, guessing at the stories behind my fellow birders. The serious ones were easy to spot, with their large binoculars and expen-sive outdoor clothing, and I mentally matched them to the license plates I'd seen in the parking lot from Colorado, Texas, and New York. Several families in parkas looked like they were locals, including a grandmotherly woman who had two bored teenagers in tow. They'd thank her for this experience one day, I hoped.

At last the cranes started to fly over our heads, first a few scattered birds and then wave after wave of them. They were headed to a roosting spot about a quarter mile downriver, heading in low over the tops of the cottonwood trees that lined the banks. Their calls—a rattling, squeaky sound like a door hinge that needs oil—grew louder and louder as the number of birds increased.

All of us on the bridge stood looking upward, enthralled by the show. Even the teenagers had dropped their air of studied boredom. Curiously, we were silent—a natural response, I think, to the wonder of what we were witnessing. By now thousands of birds were gliding across the darkening sky, their long legs trailing behind them. One flock passed by just overhead, so low that I could hear the slow, steady beat of their wings. My heart lifted in an involuntary, instinctual response, as if my soul wanted to take flight with them.

The briefest of thoughts flashed through my mind: I might get spattered with bird poop. But I quickly dismissed it, realizing it would be a small price to pay to experience the elemental power of these birds.

The ancient Greeks believed that all matter is made up of four elements: earth, water, fire, and air. Of the four, air is the most mercurial and varied, encompassing both the caress of a spring wind and the fierceness of a hurricane, the gentleness of a sleeping baby's breath and the blast of a blizzard.

Air is also invisible, which is remarkable when you think about how powerful it is. We only know about air because of its effects: a sailboat racing across water, grasses swaying, an airplane lifting off, a dog hanging out a car window so that he can smell the breeze. It's also the most essential of the elements, at least for humans. We can live without water, earth, or fire, at least for a time, but we can't last more than a few minutes without air. (Some people have trained themselves to hold their breath a little longer, but it's not a habit you can continue for very long.)

In the Bible, air is the most essential of the spiritual elements. The book of Genesis tells how God formed Adam from dirt and breathed into his nostrils the breath of life. The story uses the Hebrew *ruach*, which means "wind, breath, or spirit." This word is used almost four hundred times in the Old Testament, including in the story of creation when the spirit of God (*ruach Elohim*) hovers over the waters and when Isaiah prophesies that the spirit of the Lord (*ruach Adonai*) will rest upon the Messiah. In the New Testament, the corresponding Greek word is *pneuma*, which is used to describe the Holy Spirit. (While you want to have *pneuma*, it's best to avoid its sickly cousin *pneumonia*.) In Latin translations of the Bible, *ruach* becomes *spiritus*, from which we get *spirit*. *Inspiration*, meanwhile, comes from the Latin *inspirare*, meaning "to breathe."

The link between air and spirit continued in Christianity. Pentecost, the event that marked the beginning of the church, began with a mighty rush of wind into a room where the followers of Jesus had gathered after the resurrection. Prayers attuned to breathing were developed in the early centuries of the church and have been revived in the contemporary practice of centering prayer. And air is beloved by Christian mystics ranging from the twelfth-century abbess Hildegard of Bingen, who called herself a feather on the breath of God, to St. Francis of Assisi, who claimed Brother Wind as part of his family.

Other traditions place even more emphasis on the element of air. In Hinduism, *prana* (the Sanskrit word for breath) refers to the subtle energies that flow through all living and inanimate things, while *pranayama* is a system of breathing techniques that aid in spiritual development. The ancient Chinese tradition of Taoism has many techniques for training the breath, while Buddhism has arguably the greatest knowledge of breath practices, which undergird many of its forms of meditation.

But even if we never explore the wisdom teachings about breath or sit cross-legged on a cushion with our eyes closed, each of us has our own sacred connection to this element: our

first intake of air at birth and our last exhale at death, a perfectly symmetrical breath separated by a lifetime.

To get to Nebraska, the sandhill cranes glide on air for thousands of miles, a phenomenon repeated every spring for millennia. As one of the oldest bird species, these cranes have been
around for ten million years, and they've likely been stopping
in Nebraska on their journey ever since the Platte River was
formed at the end of the last ice age about ten thousand years
ago. Like all birds, they're descended from dinosaurs, in particular a group known as the theropods, which includes *Tyran-
nosaurus rex* as well as the smaller velociraptors. If you were
around those fierce ancestors of the cranes, you'd be worried
about much more than getting spattered with poop.

Along the Platte River, the birds find ideal conditions for
resting and gaining the weight that will sustain them for the
rest of their journey north. At night they roost on river sandbars that provide safety from predators such as coyotes, while
during the day they feast on grain left behind from the previous year's harvest as well as seeds, earthworms, snails, and
insects in the wetlands near the river.

While the sandhill cranes don't have to work very hard to
go back and forth between the Platte River and the surrounding fields, in other places they're champion flyers. With their
six-foot wingspans they can ride thermals and tail winds with
ease, covering up to five hundred miles a day and soaring to
heights of 20,000 feet or more. Other species of cranes go even
higher; some have even been observed flying over the 28,000-
foot summit of Mt. Everest.

The fact that about 80 percent of the world's sandhill crane
population converges on a seventy-five-mile section of the
Platte River each spring makes for spectacular bird watching,
but it's actually a sign of a disturbed ecosystem. The birds once
had more than two hundred miles of prime river habitat, but
today 70 percent of the water gets diverted to other uses. Wetlands have shrunk and been replaced by trees, which are much
less hospitable to cranes. Thanks to collaborations between

public entities, private landowners, and nonprofit groups, the remaining Platte River habitat is mostly protected, but it takes constant vigilance to make sure the region continues to be a haven for the birds—and by extension for the birders, who also flock here by the thousands each spring.

BIRDS OF THE SPIRIT

Just as air is associated with the spiritual realm, so are birds. Cultures around the world tell stories of birds playing the roles of messengers, role models, guardians, healers, and elders. It's said that shamans and the souls of dead people can take the form of birds and that birds carry prayers to heaven. Raptors, and eagles in particular, are regarded as sacred by many American Indian tribes, so much so that it's a felony for any non–Native American to possess eagle feathers.

In Christianity, the bird that descended upon Jesus at his baptism is a symbol of the Holy Spirit, and to this day a dove is used by countless churches in their logos, windows, and signs. John the Evangelist has traditionally been associated with the eagle, which is why some lecterns in older churches are in the form of a bird. And it's a rare person who hasn't teared up at a funeral while singing "On Eagle's Wings," a song based on Psalm 91.

I'm embarrassed to admit that before pondering the element of sacred air, I'd never made the connection between birds and angels. Think about it—angels have *wings* and *feathers*, at least in many of the images created of them through the centuries. They like to sing. They swoop in without warning. They're said to leave feathers on our paths to encourage us. About the only bird behavior they don't do is poop on people, though I would guess angel excrement could cure whatever ails you.

But among all the sacred birds, from eagles to angels, cranes hold a special place. That's especially true in many Asian cultures, where they have associations ranging from longevity and fidelity to happiness and prosperity. In ancient China, cranes were a symbol of nobility because they were believed to rule the other birds, while Taoist sages were said to be able to transform themselves into cranes. In Vietnamese mythology, cranes carry the souls of the dead to heaven; in Japan, wedding kimonos are embroidered with cranes that symbolize marital fidelity, and folding a thousand origami cranes is said to confer a wish.

Part of the reason we admire cranes is simply their appearance; their elegant, leggy beauty makes them the supermodels of the avian world. Their behaviors also intrigue us, especially their elaborate courtship rituals, which include flapping, hopping, bowing, and vocalizing in unison. Those rituals must work, because cranes remain partners for life (at least the majority do, because divorce is not unknown in the crane world). The longevity of cranes has long been admired too. They're among the longest lived of any bird species, with wild cranes often living twenty years or more.

I had my first introduction to cranes a decade ago at the International Crane Foundation in Baraboo, Wisconsin, a nonprofit that works to save the world's fifteen crane species. While the sandhill population is self-sustaining, ten of the other crane species are either endangered or threatened. From Mongolia to Mozambique, the foundation's staff is working to save these birds through research, habitat protection projects, public education, and the raising of chicks that are returned to the wild.

At the three-hundred-acre center I got the chance to see birds from all fifteen crane species, including a blue crane from southern Africa, a black-necked crane from the Himalayas, and the whooping crane, one of the most critically endangered of all bird species. They looked at me with quizzical eyes from their enclosures, these residents of an ark that seeks to save their species from the destructive forces of human thoughtlessness, greed, and development.

During my time in Nebraska, I thought back to a comment made by one of the guides at the center. "A lot of our cranes get anxious and restless around migration time in the spring and fall," she said. "Their instinct is to fly with the changing seasons, and even though they have everything they need here, they seem to sense that they're supposed to fly away."

You'd think those cranes would be grateful not to have to participate in a journey that involves traversing vast stretches of terrain, through stiff winds and occasional storms, all while having to find food and water in unfamiliar and sometimes dangerous places. Why hanker to go on such a long and dangerous journey when all your physical needs are met right where you are? The answer seems to be because that's just what cranes do.

I can sympathize with those birds, having felt that same restlessness many times in my own life. I think something similar is felt by many people. It's why we stop whatever we're doing on autumn days to look up with longing whenever we see flocks of geese honking their way across the sky. It's why those hardy souls on the footbridge were willing to brave the cold for the chance to see the cranes gliding by overhead. Maybe it's because we can hear the call of migrating birds deep in our souls, stirring an instinct that tells us to leave comfort and safety behind. It's easier to stay home, but our souls need to fly.

BREATHING IN THE SACRED

I'm in the window seat in my bedroom, hyperventilating.

Well, that's not quite right. I'm actually staring at my phone, timing my breaths to an app narrated by a man with a Dutch accent, following both his words and a set of visuals that tell me when to inhale and exhale and when to hold my breath.

"Are you OK?" Bob asks when he overhears me from another room.

"Fine!" I gasp. "Meditating!"

Bob is used to me doing weird things and doesn't bother to investigate further, which is good, because I'm already feeling self-conscious as well as stressed. I had no idea that breathing could be so hard. The relentless rhythm of fast breaths, followed by excruciatingly long periods of holding my breath, was increasing my heart rate and making me long for the exercise to be over.

I'd launched my investigation into esoteric breath practices after returning from Nebraska. As much as I'd loved watching the cranes, they'd also made me depressed that I couldn't fly with them. As an alternative, I wondered if it was possible to figuratively soar by practicing one of the methods developed thousands of years ago by people who believed that breath is our connection to spirit.

I was given an introduction to these techniques by author James Nestor, who one day wandered into a free class on Sudarshan Kriya—a form of yogic breathing—that was so powerful he spent several years trying to figure out what had happened to him. His resulting book *Breath: The New Science of a Lost Art* is a tour-de-force of everything breath-related. In it he survives doing only mouth breathing for ten days (the physical effects are ruinous), hangs out in pulmonology labs, goes exploring in the catacombs underneath Paris to discover how skulls and nasal passageways were different before the modern age, and talks to breath enthusiasts who are stretching the boundaries of what most of us think breathing can do. Along the way he cures the respiratory problems that have plagued him for most of his life. I defy anyone to read Nestor's book and not think about breathing in an entirely new way.

Nestor describes how our capacity to breathe has changed through the long processes of human evolution and how the way we breathe has gotten markedly worse since the dawn of the Industrial Age. He writes:

> [Scientists have] discovered that 90 percent of us—very likely me, you, and almost everyone you know—is breathing incorrectly and that this failure is either causing or aggravating a laundry list of chronic diseases. . . . No matter what we eat, how much we exercise, how resilient our genes are, how skinny or young or wise we are—none of it will matter unless we're breathing correctly. That's what these researchers discovered. The missing pillar in health is breath. It all starts there.

The good news is that there's solid evidence that many disorders—from asthma, anxiety, and attention deficit hyperactivity disorder to psoriasis—can either be reduced or reversed simply by changing the way we inhale and exhale. The most important thing we can do is breathe through our noses, not our mouths, because our sinuses are there for a reason—actually lots of reasons. Their passageways and cavities warm and humidify the air coming into our lungs, remove contaminants, and maintain the elasticity of the tissues at the back of our throat (the sagging of these tissues is a major cause of sleep apnea). Mouth breathing, it turns out, is one of the worst things we can do for our health.

But breathing through our noses is just the beginning of the respiration adventures that await us. There are hundreds of lesser-known breathing methods, many of which have roots in spiritual traditions. They include rapid breathing, interval breathing, and breath holding, often in complicated combinations. Many of these techniques alternate extreme stress with deep relaxation, which forces the body and mind to become more adaptable. These methods can help us reset our nervous system, control our immune response, improve our health—and advance our spiritual life, which is the part I found most intriguing.

After we had returned from Nebraska, the growing restrictions caused by the spread of COVID-19 gave me plenty of time to search the internet for breathing videos. I found lots of them, because it turns out that breathing is a thing these days. With just a click of a button, I could learn techniques that were previously taught only by gurus and meditation masters in remote corners of the world. All the instructors chirped some variation of, "Don't drive a vehicle or stand at the top of a flight of stairs while you're doing these exercises!" The reason is that you can get dizzy or even lose consciousness if you do these methods enthusiastically enough (and those with significant health issues should consult a physician before even trying them).

Even a cursory perusal of these techniques made me realize that the counting of breaths I was doing in meditation was the equivalent of riding a tricycle. I'd gotten complacent about my practice, I had to admit, proud of the fact that on most days I meditate for twenty minutes. But from the viewpoint of the Hindus practicing *pranayama*, the Taoists using breath to build *chi*, and the Tibetan Buddhists doing *tummo*, I was a rank amateur.

Take *tummo*, for instance, which in Tibetan means "inner fire." It was developed by Buddhist monks living high in the Himalayas both to propel them to a higher level of consciousness and to keep them warm, which is a good thing if you're living in a frigid, drafty monastery. Visitors to the high mountains were amazed to see *tummo* practitioners generate so much heat that they could dry wet sheets wrapped around them in freezing weather and melt the snow around them when they were sleeping. That may sound like metaphysical hype, but researchers who have studied practitioners have found that they can raise their body temperature to 101 degrees Fahrenheit.

Learning about *tummo* led me to Wim Hof, the guy who had me hyperventilating in my bedroom. Hof started investigating esoteric disciplines and the benefits of cold exposure as a way to deal with his grief after his wife's suicide in 1995. *Tummo* was one of his inspirations, though he has developed his own unique version of the practice.

Also known as the Iceman, Hof has an almost unbelievable record of physical feats, most of them relating to cold. He has run a half marathon above the Arctic Circle barefoot and in shorts, stood in a container filled with ice cubes for more than 112 minutes, and swam underneath ice for sixty-six meters. The people he's trained in his techniques have also exhibited remarkable physical changes and abilities. A study done by Radboud University in the Netherlands, for example, injected a dozen Wim Hof Method practitioners with an endotoxin derived from *E. coli* that would normally induce fever, nausea, and shivering. The Hof-trained group reacted significantly less than the control group, demonstrating for the first time that humans can voluntarily influence their autonomic nervous system and immune response.

I was fascinated by videos of a bearded, preternaturally hardy man bounding across glaciers in shorts, swimming underneath sheets of ice, meditating on the side of snowy mountains, and doing yoga poses on the edge of cliffs. Whatever his method was, it certainly seemed to be working for him. While my own motivation to try his cold-exposure therapy evaporated after my first frigid shower, his breathing method was another matter. Here was something I could do at my leisure, something that had the potential to improve my physical, mental, and spiritual well-being. And how hard could breathing be?

Well, pretty darn hard, actually. It turns out that the stress I experienced during my initial foray into the Hof method is exactly what's supposed to happen. First, I'd do rapid breathing for thirty breaths, exhale, then hold it for as long as I could, followed by an inhale and then another breath hold for fifteen seconds. That's it. Over and over. If you think that sounds easy, try it. The stress of not being able to breathe is immediate and real. Even though I knew that I could break the pattern at any time, my reptilian brain wasn't convinced.

But something started to happen as I practiced the breathing method each morning before my usual meditation session. I never developed a liking for the rapid breathing, but during the breath-holding phase of the exercise, I often experienced a laserlike focus that was startling in its clarity. When you desperately need to breathe, everything else gets stripped away, short-circuiting all the concerns that normally race through your mind. When the exercise was over, I found that I could turn to my regular quiet meditation with a sense of relief and even joy, reveling in the ease of simple respiration.

Now I realize this may sound like a highfalutin version of banging your head against a wall so you can feel how good it is to stop. But the more I practiced the Hof method, the more I gained a sense for the deep wisdom built into these seemingly simple breathing methods. My modern variation of *tummo* was helping me cope with the anxiety of living in an age of political and societal turmoil. Even more, it made me understand at a visceral level that each breath, each *ruach*, is connected to spirit. Huffing and puffing in my window seat each morning, I felt a kinship to those ancient Hebrews, Hindu yogis, and

Chinese Taoists, as well as the Tibetan monks melting snow with their meditative skills. The physical benefits of improving one's breathing are valuable, to be certain, but I could now see that the real goal in all of this is something much bigger.

It all made me think of the tornadoes that periodically sweep through my corner of the Midwest. Maybe these extreme breathing practices are like storms, bearing the same relation to normal respiration as a hurricane does to a warm spring day. Tornadoes and *tummo* aren't for the faint of heart. You can get hurt. But they also, clearly, are full of the power of air.

MORNING WITH THE CRANES

After three days in Nebraska, our time with the cranes was nearing an end. Each morning and evening we watched the birds fly back and forth from their roosting spots on the river to the fields. Despite the cold and gray weather, I never grew tired of the spectacle.

During the day we did bird-watching of another sort by driving through the back roads of the area to look for cranes feeding in the fields. With hundreds of thousands of cranes hanging around, it wasn't hard to find them. They gathered in groups ranging from a dozen birds to hundreds, walking on stiltlike legs through the stubble of cornfields, periodically stabbing their long beaks into the ground when they spied something to eat. The adults, which are about three to four feet in height, are gray with a red crown that's actually bare skin; the juveniles are more brownish and have a feathered crown. As long as we stayed in our car, they weren't bothered by us, and we spent hours observing different groups through binoculars.

I could see why their courtship dances have attracted such attention through the millennia. Suddenly in the midst of feeding a pair would start to dance, taking leaps and hops into the air with their wings partly opened, looking like slightly inebriated ballet dancers moving to music only they could hear. They bowed heads to each other, tossed pieces of vegetation up in the air, and chattered back and forth in a language only they could understand. They made being a crane look like great fun.

On our final morning, we got up even earlier than usual, packed our bags, checked out of our hotel, bought coffees at a local gas station, and headed out into the darkness. A short drive brought us to a spot on the river that had become our favorite viewing point. Then we waited, as we'd gotten used to doing. As with all wildlife watching, the animals set the schedule. Gradually the darkness began to lift, and we could see the cranes start to wake up across the river from us, hopping and calling. A few took off, getting an early start on feeding in the fields.

As the minutes passed, more and more of the birds were stirring, their cries growing in volume in the silence of the dawn. Dozens more birds effortlessly lifted off from the sandbar and headed out. Small groups passed by overhead, their calls making it seem like the birds were greeting the dawn. We sat enthralled, careful not to make a sudden move that might startle them.

But then something else spooked the cranes—perhaps a coyote or a human approaching too close. The mass of birds reacted all at once, and in the space of a minute, tens of thousands of cranes took to the skies, heading in all directions at once. The volume of their calls and the beating of their wings sounded like a freight train, a roaring that grew in intensity as more and more cranes passed by overhead, an aerial river of birds.

Bob and I stood in awed silence, tears running down our faces. The experience was unlike anything we'd experienced before. The sight was magnificent, but it was the sound that was truly overwhelming, flooding through my brain like a jolt of electricity. It was music and yet not music, harsh and yet melodious. It was the power of air distilled into one perfect experience.

It's such a cliché that I hesitate to say it, but it's true: the experience took our breath—what I now realize was our *sacred* breath—away.

The Ancient Ohio Trail includes the massive Serpent Mound, which faces the setting sun at the summer solstice. (Photo credit: Bob Sessions)

3

Mounds: The Ancient Ohio Trail

In between our visit to see the sandhill cranes and the time I visited the next holy site on my list, the world changed: the COVID-19 pandemic upended nearly everything in American society, including how I went to church.

I knew that in the context of all the tragedy going on around the world—the loss of life, the economic disruptions, the seemingly endless ripples of negative consequences spinning out from the inexorable spread of the virus—my concerns were pretty insignificant. Bob and I, thankfully, were insulated from the worst of the turmoil, tucked away in our home on a quiet residential street in Iowa, following the news with increasing anxiety but able to weather the worst of the events far better than most.

Except for church, which was like a balloon slowly losing its air, at least for me. Part of it was that while I valued my personal connections with the people in my church, I had been feeling increasingly removed from its rituals. Though I attended Sunday services when I wasn't traveling, it was more from duty than desire. When services were canceled for the first weeks of the quarantine, I welcomed the break, seeing it as a silver lining of the pandemic. Maybe when we go back to worshiping together things will be better, I thought.

But instead of meeting in person again, we switched to holding services online. At first they seemed like a relatively adequate substitute for in-person worship, but as the first few Sundays turned into a month, and then another month, and then another and another and another, my connection to my church withered even further. Seeing the array of tiny faces on my computer screen each Sunday morning just reminded me of all that we were missing—the singing of familiar hymns, the saying of the words of the liturgy in unison, the exchanging of news at coffee hour, all the minutiae of face-to-face interactions that bind a community of faith together.

As the months went on I came to actively dislike these online services, which were both too intimate and too distant—too intimate in that they put everyone just a couple of feet away from me on the screen, and too distant thanks to the awkwardness of the technology. It didn't help that I kept looking at my own face on the screen and cringing, despite my best efforts to practice self-discipline. *Why do I do that annoying thing with my mouth when I talk? I have bags under my eyes. My hair looks awful this morning. I look fake. I look too earnest. I look like I'm not paying attention. I look like I'm only pretending to pay attention.*

Other people came in for scrutiny too, especially their computer setups. Too dimly lit. Too bright. Why don't they sit closer? Why don't they sit farther away? What books are on the shelves behind them? Is that person who doesn't have her video turned on really listening, or is she only pretending to be there? And could I follow her lead?

I realized that on the spectrum of persecution that limits church attendance—exile, imprisonment, torture, being burned at the stake—having to sit in front of a computer monitor during services wasn't going to win me many extra credit points in heaven. But still—even Jesus would be challenged by online church, which is probably why he chose to come to earth before the digital age.

The central problem, I realized, is that Zoom church felt like a simulacrum of true worship, the spiritual equivalent of the uncanny valley, a term used to describe the involuntary reaction many people have to seeing simulated humans in either virtual or robotic form. Something instinctual seems to kick in, bringing with it a sense of unease and distress. Zoom church had become my uncanny valley.

At the same time, I was nearly going bonkers staying at home. For someone used to traveling regularly, the quarantine was excruciating, with each day just like the next and no end in sight. Bob and I started to take day trips, sneaking out of town without telling anyone. Going to a public restroom at a gas station felt illicit and daring, the equivalent of riding a motorcycle at ninety miles an hour without a helmet.

So when after several months of quarantine I finally planned an honest-to-goodness, out-of-town journey, what normally would have seemed like a fairly routine trip became instead a deeply significant venture into a new world. I realized that for the foreseeable future, walking sacred America wasn't just a book project but a deeply personal quest to discover the holy in a new way.

Wanting to get away from the digital world of travel planning as well as digital spirituality, I opened up a relic of another age—an actual print atlas. I flipped through its pages to find my destination, amused by how thrilled I was to be planning a trip to a place that normally doesn't inspire much romance: Ohio, that state that mirrors my own home of Iowa in both its number of vowels and its ho-hum reputation in the larger world. But I had a sense that Ohio was where I needed to go next, and that it just might have holy sites as significant as any in the world.

OHIO'S JERUSALEM

If you've never heard of the Ancient Ohio Trail, you're not alone. But this relatively unknown route links sites that are among the world's most significant prehistoric landmarks. Most are on or adjacent to the Appalachian Plateau, a rugged region on the western side of the Appalachian Mountains. The most significant sites are Newark, the largest set of geometric earthworks in the world; Mound City, which holds an ancient necropolis; Fort Ancient, the largest hilltop enclosure in North America; and most intriguing of all, Serpent Mound, a massive earthen snake that faces the setting sun at the summer solstice.

"These landmarks are as remarkable as the Egyptian pyramids or Stonehenge," said Brad Lepper, the senior archaeologist for the Ohio History Connection's World Heritage Program. "The technology used to build them was simple—just pointed sticks, clamshell hoes, and woven baskets—but the knowledge encoded in these monuments is extraordinarily sophisticated."

In preparation for my journey I'd contacted Brad, who has devoted his career to studying the prehistoric mound-building cultures of Ohio. In a phone interview, he gave me an introduction to the Hopewell Culture, which flourished between 1 and 400 CE. Because the original name of these people is unknown, archeologists have designated them as the Hopewell, after Mordecai Hopewell, who owned the farm where one of the earthworks was excavated in 1891.

When I asked Brad for his recommendation for where to start my tour, he didn't hesitate. "Go to Newark," he said. "It was the Mecca, the Jerusalem, of the Hopewell world. If you want to try to understand the Hopewell, you need to start there."

A couple of weeks later as Bob and I drove into Newark, however, it didn't look much like a holy site. Instead, this small city located thirty miles east of Columbus had a familiar mix of fast-food outlets, shopping malls, and residential streets. Then I remembered a map I'd studied in advance of my visit, one created in the mid-1800s when this area was first filling with white settlers. Realizing that thousands of prehistoric mounds were being irreparably damaged, Ephraim George Squier and Edwin Hamilton Davis, both from the Ohio town of Chillicothe, undertook one of the most significant scientific endeavors in the history of the United States. Working in collaboration with the then-fledgling Smithsonian Institution, the two surveyed all the known earthworks in the middle of the country. Their work became *Ancient Monuments of the Mississippi Valley*, which in 1848 became the first book published by the Smithsonian. Its beautifully detailed maps and diagrams are a guide to ancient treasures, most of which have been lost to farming and urban development.

Primed by my conversation with Brad Lepper, I'd pored over the portion of the book relating to Newark. The maps drawn by Squier and Davis helped me understand that underneath the veneer of the modern city were the remains of a four-square-mile complex of earthworks that included massive circles, a huge square, and a precisely engineered octagon, all connected by walled roadways. The geometric forms—constructed from an estimated seven million cubic feet of earth—reminded me of the circuit board of a computer, as anachronistic as that analogy seems for a civilization that existed two millennia ago.

Fortunately, several of the major Hopewell creations in Newark have been preserved, including the Great Circle, which is protected as a National Historic Landmark in the middle of the city. After parking our car in a small lot next to the circle, we started walking along a fourteen-foot-tall, grass-covered earthen wall that curved into the distance in both directions. Coming to the monument's only entryway, a gap in the eastern side of the wall, we got our first clear view inside. At first glance it seemed like an ordinary park, with a carpet of green grass and scattered trees. But as we walked farther into its interior, the full scale of the Great Circle became apparent. Twelve hundred feet in diameter, it's so large that four football fields could fit within it. I remembered reading that in 1874 when Newark hosted a reunion of Civil War veterans, more than twenty thousand people gathered inside of the Great Circle with room to spare. As much as I loved the bear effigies in northeastern Iowa, this was an earthen monument on an entirely different scale.

"Amazing!" Bob exclaimed. "This is cooler than I expected, given what you said about it."

I'd deliberately downplayed what we would see, having learned my lesson long ago on a trip we took to Scotland with our sons when they were kids. For weeks I'd built up the prospect of seeing Hadrian's Wall, which was built by the Roman army in the second century to protect themselves from attack by the native peoples of the north. "You will love it!" I told them. "It's one of the wonders of Britain. And there's nothing cooler than Roman soldiers and Celtic warriors!"

Instead, our tour of Hadrian's Wall was thoroughly miserable. The weather was cold and rainy with a stiff wind, and as we walked along a segment of the wall, Owen and Carl were distinctly unimpressed.

"This is it?" Owen said, looking like I'd taken away his Christmas presents. "Some rocks?"

"You said this was going to be interesting," Carl chimed in. "It's just a broken-down old wall."

I decided that in Ohio it would be better to err on the side of understatement, because while Bob has great patience and considerable enthusiasm when he joins me on research trips, even he has his limits. I knew that like Hadrian's Wall, the mounds don't have the star power of showy landmarks like pyramids or cathedrals. Instead, they take some imagination, which has always struck me as an underappreciated part of the spiritual path.

We ventured farther into the circle. I could see the ditch on the interior of its walls, an eight-foot-deep depression that had originally been lined with clay and limestone so that it could hold water. Given its size and position, the ditch probably was created for ceremonial or symbolic reasons rather than practical ones. Another curious feature was a rounded hill at the circle's center known as Eagle Mound. An excavation in 1928 found a ceremonial longhouse beneath it, a building with two walls projecting from its eastern end like wings. The amount of effort required to build all of these structures, especially given the simple technology of the period, is staggering.

"This took a huge amount of work," Bob said, "especially without bulldozers."

"Just wait till you see what's coming next," I told him, daring to venture a little bit of an advertisement for what was coming next.

"Where are we going?"

"A golf course," I replied. "But it's not your typical golf course."

I wasn't kidding. Our next site on the Ancient Ohio Trail was the Moundbuilders Country Club, which has its golf links and putting greens inside two major landmarks built by the Hopewell. Negotiations are underway to transfer the land to the Ohio History Connection, but in the meantime this is the only holy site I know of where you need to watch out for stray golf balls.

An observation platform near the clubhouse gave us a panoramic view of two earthworks that eclipse the Great Circle in size and probably in original importance. The first, known as the Observatory Circle, has a diameter of 1,050 feet, while the other is the Octagon, an eight-sided figure more than 1,500 feet across. Linked by a narrow avenue, the two are a matched set. Once again, the scale of the monument was difficult to comprehend. Four structures the size of the Roman Coliseum could fit inside the Octagon alone. Taken together, the two stretch for half a mile, with earthen walls ranging between three and seven feet tall.

As I surveyed the monuments, I tried to imagine them during the time of the Hopewell, when these sites were linked to the Great Circle by a mile-long walled avenue. Once inside the complex of earthworks, people would have been directed from one grand ceremonial space to the next. I could see why archaeologists believe the Newark earthworks were a pilgrimage destination for a large region, because the monuments are much bigger than a local group would have needed.

Even more impressive is that these spaces were built not just in precise geometric patterns but also according to astronomical alignments—and not to the sun, which is relatively easy to track, but instead to the moon, which is far more capricious in its movements. In addition to waxing and waning, the moon's rising point on the horizon swings back and forth between the southeast and northeast about every four weeks. The angle of its transit across the sky slowly expands over a period of about nine years and then contracts at the same rate. The result is that there are eight points where the moon seems to reverse direction—and at the Newark Octagon, all of these eight points are marked by alignments with earthen walls and gateways.

The longest cycle is the northernmost rise of the moon, which happens once every 18.6 years. On that night, if you're standing in the center of the Observatory Circle and look directly through the avenue that connects to the Octagon, you will see the moon rise serenely in perfect alignment with the earthworks, just as the Hopewell did many centuries ago. These people didn't just move piles of earth—they figured out how the earth itself is related to its companion the moon.

It's a phenomenon that still stirs the hearts of observers, including Brad Lepper when he experienced the northernmost moonrise at Hopewell for the first time in 2006. "I can't tell you how amazing it was to be a student of the Hopewell Culture and to stand in the Observatory Circle and watch the moon rise along this axis just as those people did two thousand years ago," Brad recalled. "The hair on the back of my neck stood up. This is a cosmic alarm clock that was wound up two millennia ago, and it still works."

I watched a lone golfer walking across the grass inside the Octagon, wondering if he had any sense of the importance of the landmark he was traversing.

SUPERCONDUCTORS OF THE SACRED

The golfers at the Moundbuilders Country Club have grown accustomed to the earthworks all around them, but to the first Europeans who ventured into the Mississippi and Ohio River valleys in the 1700s, the thousands of seemingly abandoned mounds they encountered were a mystery. The native peoples of the region knew little about them, which led some of the new residents to speculate that the mounds were built by a "lost race" that had vanished before the contemporary Native Americans arrived on the scene. Other settlers believed they'd been built by giants, the same creatures known as Nephilim in the book of Genesis. ("I still get questions about giants at many of the public talks I give," Brad Lepper told me with a sigh.)

Over the past century, archaeological research has helped unravel at least some of the mysteries of the mounds. Their builders were primarily hunter-gatherers who lived in small homesteads in the surrounding region, not at the earthworks themselves. The archaeological record indicates that unlike other prehistoric cultures that constructed large monuments, they didn't have a complex social hierarchy involving nobles supported by peasants or slaves, which suggests that building the mounds was a voluntary communal project.

Why did they put so much effort and care into constructing these landmarks? We'll never know for certain, but Brad Lepper makes an educated guess about what happened at Newark. "I think there may have been a charismatic leader who came up with the design and got people interested in building these huge earthen structures in precise patterns," he said. "Other sites in the region were built over many years, but I think Newark was built over a relatively short period of time. The Newark sites might have been a kind of ceremonial machine that synthesized all they'd been developing in the larger region for generations. You could think of them as the Hopewell equivalent of our giant supercolliders, monumental machinery designed to unleash powerful cosmic forces."

While most of us today are largely disconnected from the rhythms of nature, Brad's words made me realize that for much of human existence the heavens were an intimate part of people's ordinary lives, viewed each night above the dancing light of campfires. It's not surprising that some people began to keep records of what they observed, in part because accurate calendars helped them make decisions relating to planting and harvesting. But while keeping track of the sun's movements

clearly has useful applications, paying attention to the mean-
dering multiyear cycle of the moon seems less practical and
more mystical, at least in my view. And at Newark, those lunar
alignments seemed to be an important part of the grand ceremonial landscape from the very beginning.

Even before the advent of modern science, many cultures
throughout history deduced that heavenly bodies move in
recurring patterns. Ancient civilizations that included the
Egyptians, Greeks, and Mayans incorporated sacred geometry
into their architecture, trying to replicate in their holy sites
the divine symmetry they observed in the heavens. Christianity has its own versions of sacred geometry, most visible in the
mathematical symmetries and symbolic architectural elements
of medieval cathedrals. By praying and worshiping in structures like these, people of many eras and belief systems hoped
to connect with spiritual forces.

In my travels around the world, I've seen the sacred expressed
in many forms, from music and dance to calligraphy and even
tattoos. But geometry? That high school class that made my
eyes glaze over? If God is indeed a mathematician, I had a lot
to learn.

The next site we visited is just a baby by Hopewell standards,
but its significance belies its modest size.

Located sixty miles southwest of Newark on the outskirts
of the city of Chillicothe, Mound City is the centerpiece of
the Hopewell Culture National Historical Park. The park preserves six noncontiguous sites, five of which echo the Newark
fascination with circles, squares, and octagons. While those
landmarks exist only in fragmented form, the Mound City
site has been restored to its original appearance. Twenty-three
mounds, the largest of which is about seventeen feet in height
and ninety in diameter, fill a thirteen-acre rectangle bounded
by a low earthen wall. Most of the mounds are dome-shaped,
making the site look like a bunch of anthills left by giant insects.

If Newark might have been the equivalent of Jerusalem for
the Hopewell, Mound City was the place where their most

important leaders were buried, a version of the memorial shrines inside Westminster Abbey or the monuments that line the Mall in Washington, D.C. The mounds cover the remains of ceremonial buildings where cremations occurred, with the ashes placed beneath the floor. After being used multiple times, the structures were burned and the remains covered with earthen mounds.

"About a hundred people were buried here over a period of several centuries," explained the park ranger who greeted me outside the visitor center. "These were likely the most revered members of the Hopewell culture, people they wanted to honor with special ceremonies and grave goods."

I told her how impressed I'd been by the sites at Newark and that I was surprised the Hopewell sites aren't better known. "We hope that will change if these sites get designated as UNESCO World Heritage Sites," she said. "We're on the short list for approval, so the odds are good. But even if we get that designation, I think it's difficult for people to fully appreciate the Hopewell sites because they were built of earth, not stone. Farming and development have taken a big toll, and our climate works against us too, with a lot of rain and weathering. You have to work to understand the significance of what we have here."

As Bob and I set out to explore the burial mounds, I thought back to the holy dirt of Chimayó. The builders of the Ohio monuments also made use of soil, though their dirt was hauled and shaped, not just gathered from nearby hills. I wondered what the Hopewell builders thought as they engaged in their difficult labor. Through their prodigious efforts, they in a sense incorporated their own selves into the mounds, blending their sweat with the soil.

The building skills of the Hopewell are reflected not only in the geometric precision of the monuments but also in how they used different types of soil depending upon the type of structure they were building. Sometimes the soil was layered with dirt of different colors, sometimes it was mixed with sand and gravel to increase drainage, and other times it was lined with clay to hold water. These prehistoric builders reminded me of the stonemasons who worked on the medieval cathedrals of Europe, each contributing to a structure they might never see finished but that they hoped would long outlive them.

Christianity doesn't do much with the idea of sacred mounds; in fact, such landmarks have often been viewed with suspicion. The prehistoric barrow mounds of the British Isles, for example, have long been associated with eerie supernatural forces. But the Ohio mounds didn't seem threatening to me. Instead, they have an air of faded grandeur, like the ruins of churches long abandoned. And even though I didn't know what rituals were done there or what belief system undergirded them, I felt a sense of kinship with the people who built them.

The next day we toured Fort Ancient in southern Ohio, another site that showcases the Hopewell enthusiasm for moving huge amounts of dirt. On a high plateau above the Little Miami River are nearly three and a half miles of earthen embankments enclosing about a hundred acres. While the first Europeans who came across the site likely dubbed it a fort because of its resemblance to the ancient hill forts of western Europe, the hilltop enclosure almost certainly wasn't built for defensive purposes. One clue is that it has nearly seventy openings in its walls—not very sensible if you're trying to keep invaders out. As at the other sites, we don't know what the Hopewell were up to, but we do know it took enormous effort.

Of the sites we'd visited, this one took the most imagination to appreciate. (Hadrian's Wall came to mind, in fact.) While some parts of the hilltop enclosure were visible, most of it looked like natural landforms covered with trees and bushes. Thankfully, the site's museum fleshed out additional parts of the Hopewell story. Exhibits describe the finely crafted artifacts these people left behind, items made with mica from the Carolinas, copper from the upper Great Lakes, shells from the Gulf of Mexico, and obsidian from Yellowstone National Park. It's not known how these exotic materials ended up here. Perhaps they were trade goods or the offerings of pilgrims who traveled from afar to experience the awe-inspiring monuments. Or maybe people from this region visited distant lands and brought back intriguing new materials that were shaped into high-status objects.

Peering into the display cases, I thought about several additional items I knew are kept at the Ohio History Center in Columbus and at Mound City. These superstar artifacts include a hand with strangely elongated fingers formed from shimmering mica, a figurine of a man wearing a bear headdress and holding a human head in his lap, and a copper rendering of the hallucinogenic amanita mushroom. (That last one might explain where the Hopewell got some of the inspiration for building their earthworks.)

The museum's exhibits also describe how in the sixth century the Hopewell culture faded, to be followed by the Fort Ancient culture (which is confusing because the actual Fort Ancient was built by the Hopewell, a historical mistake that's enshrined in the name). This latter group relied more on agriculture than hunting and gathering, and their society was more structured and hierarchical. Instead of building the large geometric structures favored by the Hopewell, their mounds tended to be smaller and were sometimes in the shape of animals.

Then the Fort Ancient culture faded as well. By the early 1600s the effects of Europeans arriving in North America were increasingly widespread, especially in the diseases that had spread across the continent. It's estimated that up to 90 percent of the native population of North America died after being exposed to diseases for which they had no immunity. It's no wonder, then, that by the time white settlers began arriving in great numbers in the eighteenth and nineteenth centuries, the remaining native tribes of the Ohio region knew little about the mounds.

I thought of the spread of COVID-19 across the world in my own day, a much less deadly disease than those faced by the native peoples of the Americas after European contact. But even this milder virus had wreaked havoc with entire nations, giving me a small glimpse of the terror and devastation experienced by the Indigenous peoples of the post-Columbian era. So much was lost, including a living memory of the mound-building cultures of their ancestors.

Thankfully, today the descendants of the Fort Ancient people—who include members of the Shawnee, the Miami, and the Osage tribes—have reclaimed a connection to the prehistoric landmarks. They work with the Ohio History Connection to present educational programming on the Native American heritage of the mounds. And while the various tribes acknowledge that no one can say exactly why these places were built or how they were used, they affirm that they are holy places deserving of great respect.

THE SERPENT IN SEARCH OF THE SUN

At last it was time to visit the most intriguing mound of them all: the Great Serpent, which winds its way down a hill in rural Ohio near the small town of Peebles. While the Hopewell sites require some imagination to appreciate, this landmark—a quarter mile in length—elicits an instinctual response. Snakes have that power, even in earthen form.

I'd seen pictures of the Serpent Mound before arriving at the site, but nothing prepared me for my first full view of it. Surrounded by forest, the snake's undulating curves have a beauty and gracefulness that make the landmark seem as much a work of art as a prehistoric landmark. Brad Lepper had told me that the first time he visited there, he felt like he was in a church. I knew exactly what he meant, because I sensed something I've felt at other great religious landmarks—that the veil between worlds is thin here.

Resisting the urge to immediately explore the mound, I headed to the visitor center for some background that would help me understand it better. There I learned that the dating of the Serpent Mound, the largest effigy mound in the world, is less certain than that of the other Ohio earthworks. The archaeological evidence is conflicting, suggesting that it was built either about 900 or 2,300 years ago, though it's also possible that the site was periodically refurbished and renewed throughout its existence. While the Hopewell likely didn't construct it, the mound is another example of the earth-moving creativity of the prehistoric peoples of Ohio.

At the visitor center I spoke with Beth Jenkins, historic site group lead for Serpent Mound. She told me that this is still an active pilgrimage destination, a living holy site much more than the other sites we'd visited in Ohio. "Most of our visitors know that this is a sacred American Indian site, though people have a variety of beliefs about it," she said. "Some visitors think it has something to do with aliens or ghosts. Many people associate it with healing. I'm a historian, so I'm most interested in what can be known from archaeological research. But I also think it's up to individuals to decide what this place means to them. I do think it's interesting that it's been a popular place for reunions of Ohio families for many generations. Something about this place just draws people in."

Not surprisingly, the most popular time to visit the mound is at the summer solstice, when the sun sets in alignment with the mouth of the snake. The site's solstice observance typically draws about four thousand visitors. "A lot of people see the solstice as a time of renewal, and they come here to celebrate new beginnings in their own lives," Beth said.

I imagined Ohio's version of the modern-day Druids who gather at England's Stonehenge at the solstices, picturing their tie-dye T-shirts and flowing scarves. It's easy to make fun of such people, but on my travels I've come to have a great deal of respect for these fellow spiritual travelers, who can be a bit quirky but who often have a deep connection to the earth's wonders. Of course they are drawn to this giant snake that slithers its way through the Ohio hills. I'd be disappointed in them if they weren't.

And as if it's not enough to be oriented to the summer solstice, I learned that there's another unusual aspect to this landmark: it sits inside an impact crater created by a meteor approximately 300 million years ago. It's one of eighteen known impact craters in the United States. While the five-mile gash in the earth would have long been covered by vegetation by the time the mound was constructed, the rock beneath the surface is much different from that of the surrounding region, its layers compressed and twisted by the force of the impact. Both a snake *and* a meteor crater? This holy site hits the spiritual jackpot.

After hearing in the visitor center that compasses can behave oddly around impact craters, I bought a compass in the gift shop before setting out on my own explorations. Then I headed out the door, lost in thought, only to give an involuntary jump when I saw a large snake slithering across the path in front of me. Four feet long and black, it was taking its time as it moved, not fazed by the small group of people that had gathered excitedly around it.

"Oh, that's Oliver," said Beth from behind me, having come out to investigate the commotion. "He lives around here. During the winter when we're closed we let him stay in the visitor center. He likes to sleep in the display case near the cash register."

I watched as Oliver disappeared, intrigued by the synchronicity of having seen an actual snake at the Serpent Mound, like a wink from an invisible storyteller who was spinning a deeper tale than I realized.

The information I'd learned swirled through my head as I headed to the Serpent Mound and began walking the paved trail that encircles its length. Up close, I could see that the snake's coils are about three feet in height (although they were likely a foot or two higher before gravity and weathering took their toll). At the head, I pondered the oval enclosed by the serpent's mouth, a rounded form that's been variously interpreted as an egg, an eye, or the sun, among many other suggestions. A few yards more and I peered downward through the thick vegetation below the cliff edge, trying to spy the rock outcropping that's said to resemble a serpent's head, which might have influenced why the monument was built on this site.

I thought of Brad Lepper's comment that visiting here makes him feel like he's in a church. A Serpent Church—now that's an unusual concept, at least for most Christians. Except for fundamentalist snake handlers, we don't associate reptiles with churches. In fact, Christianity has had a pretty dysfunctional relationship with snakes, given the story of what happened in the Garden of Eden. In Christian iconography, holy figures often step with great relish on the heads of serpents, proof that a grudge is still borne.

But many cultures have much more positive views of these creatures. Because snakes appear to die before being reborn in a new skin, they're often associated with death and resurrection. The Tantric traditions of India believe that a serpentine energy known as kundalini lies at the base of our spines, a power that can be awakened in meditation so that it rises up our bodies in a burst of ecstasy. In classical Greece, the divine healer Asclepius carried a staff with a serpent coiled around it. To this day, the Rod of Asclepius is used as a symbol of the field of medicine.

More direct links to the Great Serpent Mound may exist in the many stories told by Native American tribes about serpents with great powers, creatures that are mostly benevolent but sometimes evil. In particular, Serpent Mound may be connected to a story told by the ancestors of the modern-day Quapaw, Osage, Kansas, Ponca, and Omaha tribal nations, in which First Woman had intercourse with the Great Serpent and from him gained the power to resurrect herself.

As I started my return walk along the serpent's other side, the shifting light from passing clouds played across its coils in a way that made them seem almost as if they were moving. I'd never been at a holy site quite as uncanny in its beauty. It's not surprising, I thought, that some people report strange dreams after visiting here, and I wondered what I might dream of that night. Like so many spiritual sites I've visited around the globe, this place seemed to have the power to reflect and amplify the spirit in mysterious ways.

On my slow walk around the perimeter of the serpent, I periodically checked the compass I'd purchased at the visitor center. To my disappointment, the needle always pointed north—until suddenly the needle shifted ninety degrees. It continued that way for several yards, then shifted back. A few yards later, it happened again.

Now I realize this likely had something to do with the layers of earth below me having been changed by the meteor impact, as my source at the visitor center had indicated. A shift in a local magnetic field isn't that unusual, even in places that didn't receive such a shake-up. But still, I was thrilled to see it happening as I walked. I guessed that the builders of the mound, those connoisseurs of soil, sensed that something was different underneath the surface of this ground.

As for me, that wandering compass needle struck me as a metaphor for what was happening in my spiritual life as I walked the sacred sites of America. My mother's death had unmoored me more than I realized, a loss deepened by the turmoil caused by COVID-19 and the fracturing of my church community. It felt as if my internal compass had been reoriented along the Ancient Ohio Trail, making me more attuned than ever before to the wonders below my feet.

Mark Pederson has been working in the quarries at Minnesota's Pipestone National Monument for more than forty years. (PHOTO CREDIT: NPS/J. BORDEN)

4

Stone: Pipestone National Monument in Minnesota

The COVID-19 pandemic continued, but so did our travels. Our tiny teardrop camper—so cute that it was a rare day when no one asked for our one-minute tour of it—made it possible for us to travel relatively safely. By now, entering a public restroom had lost some of its feeling of danger. The virus was here to stay, but we would try to dodge an encounter with it on our mission to explore sacred sites in America.

Our next stop was a place where I wanted to explore how stones can be holy: Pipestone National Monument in southwestern Minnesota, where for more than three thousand years Native Americans have been quarrying rock used to make ceremonial pipes. Its deposits of red stone are said to contain the blood of the ancestors of Indigenous people.

Among the sacred elements I hoped to explore, I had to admit that stones were a stretch. In New Mexico I'd felt the power of sacred dirt, and Ohio's sacred mounds had completely won me over. But stones? I'm interested in almost everything except sports and geology, I've sometimes told Bob, who in contrast to me is a stone lover from way back. He picks up rocks in nearly every place we travel, so that by the end of a trip his backpack weighs nearly as much as his suitcase. Most of his finds end up in our garden, except for one stone from a beach in Whitby, England, that he kept in his pocket for nearly twenty years before it finally disappeared, no doubt weary from all the traveling.

While Bob's not known for the keenness of his spiritual radar, he has a sense that the stones are more than just a reminder of the places we've been. "Certain stones reach out to me," he says. "It sounds weird, but it's true."

As for me, stones haven't ranked high in my metaphysical musings. I hoped that Pipestone could teach me what I was missing.

We arrived at Pipestone National Monument on a warm summer morning. I'd been to this spot a dozen years before, but I was eager to see it through new eyes. Before, I was a tourist; now I was a pilgrim, and that made all the difference in how I approached this landscape.

At the monument's visitor center I met park ranger Gabrielle Drapeau, who introduced herself as a member of the Yankton Sioux Tribe. "My family has deep roots in this region," she said. "I started volunteering at Pipestone as a teenager and after college was fortunate to be hired as a ranger. I love sharing my heritage with visitors, especially ones who are open to the spirit of this place."

While Bob headed off to take pictures, Gabrielle and I set out on a paved trail that led us through a grassland filled with blooming flowers and twittering birds. As we walked, Gabrielle told me that Pipestone is affiliated with twenty-three tribal nations, each of which has its own traditions relating to ceremonial pipes, the quarries, and pipestone itself. The connecting thread between all of them is that this has long been considered a sacred place.

"In my own tradition, we believe that the red in the pipestone is the blood of our people," she explained. "Our elders tell the story that many years ago there was a terrible flood, and the blood from those who died seeped down into the rock. When we come here, we connect with our ancestors."

Gabrielle said that while Pipestone National Monument was established in 1937 to preserve the quarries, it also protects another treasure: the tallgrass prairie ecosystem that we were walking through, one that's changed little since prehistoric times. Only a fraction remains of these grasslands that once covered vast stretches of North America. Pipestone's prairie has more than five hundred species of plants, many of which have been used for food and medicine by the native peoples of the region. As we walked, Gabrielle pointed out wild bergamot and purple coneflowers, both of which have a variety of medicinal uses.

A few minutes later we approached the first quarry, an area of exposed rock about fifteen feet across, ten feet long, and six feet deep. The monument has fifty-six small quarries like this scattered across a seam of pipestone that runs through its 301 acres. Quarrying permits are given only to members of federally recognized tribes, and all the work must be done by hand.

"When you're in the quarries, you have to work really hard to get down to the pipestone layer," said Gabrielle, who is learning the process from those who've worked in the quarries for years. "It can take many weeks to reach the thin layer of pipestone, which is under four to ten feet of Sioux quartzite. You're using pry bars, wedges, and sledgehammers on stone that's harder than granite."

Peering down into the pit, I could see tools propped against a rock and the three-foot-deep layer of Sioux quartzite that lies atop a thin layer of pipestone. Gabrielle was right—it would certainly take an enormous amount of work to extract the sacred stone by hand.

Gabrielle next shared the geological story of the monument. More than a billion years ago, a river deposited thousands of feet of sand in this region. Then came a layer of clay, followed by thousands more feet of sand. Over millennia, pressure and heat compacted the layers, with the sand forming the Sioux quartzite layers and the clay mixture compacted into the pipestone layer. The pipestone was called catlinite by geologists, in honor of George Catlin, an artist whose 1836 paintings of the quarries stirred national interest. The pipestone layer—which is ten to eighteen inches deep—is actually composed of smaller, fragile sheets of rock only one and a half to three inches thick. While it takes brute force to get through the quartzite, great delicacy is needed to remove the pipestone.

"There are other pipestone deposits around North America," said Gabrielle, "but the rock from these quarries is especially prized for its beauty and quality."

I had to admit that the scientific explanation didn't interest me nearly as much as Gabrielle's earlier story of the blood of her people in the rocks. But I liked how Pipestone National Monument tells both stories. Those who are comfortable with paradox and mystery have no trouble believing that both stories are true.

As we continued walking, I felt keenly that I was just a visitor there, even more than I'd felt at the Ohio sites. Seeing Gabrielle's love for this sacred place was humbling, making me realize that I could never fully understand what this place means to the people whose ancestors have been working the quarries for millennia. But thanks to her guidance, I was already looking at the landscape differently because of knowing what lies beneath the surface of the grasses and flowers that swayed in the warm summer wind.

The winding path brought us to a cliff wall and scattered outcroppings of exposed Sioux quartzite, which has a pinkish hue. More than 1.6 billion years old, it's one of the world's oldest and hardest rocks. While pipestone is not used for buildings because of its softness, quartzite is a popular building material in the region. Driving through the town of Pipestone on our way to the monument, we'd passed many buildings constructed from it.

Next we came to Pipestone Creek and lovely Winnewissa Falls, whose waters form an oasis of green vegetation in the middle of the drier prairie. On the trees and bushes growing amid the rocks I could see prayer offerings in the form of ribbons and small bundles of sacred herbs. Gabrielle explained that people from many tribal nations come great distances to attend ceremonies and pray at the monument as well as work in the quarries. Sun dances, sweat lodges, and vision quests are held on parts of the monument that are off-limits to the general public.

"But all of this place is sacred," she concluded. "I feel especially connected to this land because of my ancestors, but I think everyone who comes here can feel the sacredness of this place if their hearts are open."

As we completed our tour and walked back to the visitor center, I realized I was beginning to better understand the power of sacred stone.

THE GIFT OF WHITE BUFFALO CALF WOMAN

In a time of famine, a woman dressed in white buckskin appeared out of nowhere on the Great Plains: White Buffalo Calf Woman. According to Lakota tradition she was *wakȟáŋ*, meaning she possessed great spiritual power. After teaching the Lakota people the rituals relating to the sacred pipe and how to follow a path in harmony with the earth, she promised to return again to them at some point in the future, and then began to walk away. After a short distance she sat upon the ground, and when she rose up again she became first a red-and-brown buffalo calf, then a white buffalo, and then a black buffalo before finally disappearing over a hill. To this day a white buffalo is considered the most sacred of animals to the Lakota.

The story comes from *The Sacred Pipe: Black Elk's Account of the Seven Rites of the Oglala Sioux,* a book suggested to me by Gabrielle. Black Elk, an Oglala Lakota visionary and healer, gave this testimony to Joseph Epes Brown, who recorded and edited the transcripts into a volume published in 1953. Black Elk's book begins with the story of how White Buffalo Calf

Woman taught the sacred pipe traditions to the Lakota, an indication of how important they are to his people.

While I loved the entire book, these words in particular from White Buffalo Calf Woman spoke to me:

> With this sacred pipe you will walk upon the Earth; for the Earth is your Grandmother and Mother, and She is sacred. Every step that is taken upon Her should be as a prayer. The bowl of this pipe is of red stone; it is the Earth. Carved in the stone and facing the center is this buffalo calf who represents all the four-leggeds who live upon your Mother. The stem of the pipe is of wood, and this represents all that grows upon the Earth. And these twelve feathers which hang here where the stem fits into the bowl are from *Wanbli Galeshka*, the Spotted Eagle, and they represent the eagle and all the wingeds of the air. All these peoples, and all the things of the universe, are joined to you who smoke the pipe—all send their voices to Wakan-Tanka, the Great Spirit. When you pray with this pipe, you pray for and with everything.

That image of prayer enfolding everything, of the smoke rising from the pipe uniting the four directions and the earth and the sky and the animals, spoke to something deep in my heart. I realized once again how spiritually isolated I felt during the pandemic, both from my fellow parishioners and from a sense of the sacred. Hearing about this tradition so deeply rooted in the earth felt like rain upon a parched landscape.

The White Buffalo Calf Woman story is just one of many traditions relating to sacred pipes in North America, many of which originated at Pipestone. Because the Minnesota stone is both beautiful and relatively easy to carve, before European contact it was traded widely throughout the continent. I was pleased to learn that pipes made from stone quarried in Minnesota have even been found in Hopewell burial sites—another example of the threads that seemed to connect many of the holy sites I was visiting. I wondered if the Hopewell had used them in ceremonies held during that once-in-a-generation northernmost moonrise.

In the mid-nineteenth century, the millennia-old traditions at the quarries were gravely threatened when white settlers began arriving in great numbers. As in many other places in the United States, tensions grew between the native peoples and those who sought to displace them from their land. A Yankton chief named Struck By The Ree visited Washington, D.C., in 1857 on behalf of his people, trying to devise a path of peaceful coexistence. After the U.S. government drafted a treaty that would place the Yankton nation on a reservation 150 miles away, Struck By The Ree refused to sign it unless his people were granted use of the Pipestone quarries. His efforts are credited with the establishment of the one-square-mile reservation that protected the sacred land and the right of American Indians to quarry there.

The agreement that saved the quarries was a rare victory in the waves of tragedy that engulfed native peoples across the continent. Over the next decades, most were forced to leave their homelands and move onto reservations. Beginning in the late nineteenth century, this tragedy was compounded by the practice of forcibly enrolling Indigenous children in boarding schools. The Pipestone Indian Training School, which operated from 1893 to 1953, was one of many institutions in which children were forbidden to speak their native languages, cut off from their cultural and spiritual roots, and forced to assimilate to mainstream American culture. Many were also physically, emotionally, and sexually abused. It was a bitter irony indeed to have an Indian school at the sacred site of Pipestone.

It is a testimony to native resilience, strength, and persistence that the quarrying traditions were not lost during these years of oppression. And in the 1970s, the rise of Indigenous activist groups helped spur renewed interest in traditional spiritual practices, a renaissance that has continued. Today Pipestone has once again taken its rightful place as one of the most significant Indigenous holy sites in America. In the quarries, the pounding of hammers is the heartbeat of a living tradition.

Sacred pipes have often been misunderstood by outsiders. In the eighteenth and nineteenth centuries they were often called "peace pipes" by American settlers and soldiers, who saw them being smoked to mark treaty signings. They didn't realize that the pipes were used in many settings, from preparing for battle and rites of passage to communal and personal prayer.

One of the most popular styles is the calumet, which is a T-shaped pipe with a bowl of stone and a wooden stem. It may be simple or adorned with carvings, feathers, beadwork, quills, or fur. Some pipes have been passed down from generation to generation for hundreds of years. In most tribes, the role of pipe-keeper is one of great honor and responsibility.

Because of their sacred nature the Pipestone visitor center does not sell pipes, but its store stocks other crafts made from pipestone, from effigies of turtles to bowls for the burning of sage, which is used for purification. On my previous visit to the monument, I'd watched as an artisan crafted a piece of pipe-stone, rubbing it with sandpaper as we talked. She said that after she finished shaping it, she would heat the stone and then rub beeswax on it to bring out its deep red color. I'd held one of her finished pieces in my hand and rubbed its surface with my finger, pleased by its smooth-as-silk feel.

Visiting the monument a second time deepened my under-standing of sacred stone, especially its connection to prayer. Gabrielle told me that pipe ceremonies still include prayers to the four directions, the earth, and the sky, just as White Buf-falo Calf Woman had taught them long ago. Bits of kinnick-kinnick (an herbal mixture made from local plants) are added to the bowl with each of these prayers so that when the pipe is smoked, it's believed that all of creation comes together in the prayers that waft upward to the Great Spirit.

"The bowl and stem are always stored separately and are only put together when the pipe is going to be used," Gabrielle told me. "You hold the bowl in your left hand and the stem in your right. When they are put together they become a living being."

I realized I'd already encountered evidence of the sacred pipe tradition in the many historical paintings and photographs I'd seen of Indigenous leaders who hold a calumet, though I hadn't realized its full significance until now. One picture in particular stood out: an image of the revered Hunkpapa Lakota leader Sitting Bull gazing directly at the camera, a pipe cradled gently in his arms like it was a precious child. After being at Pipestone, I could understand why he held it with such reverence.

PRAYER PARTNERS OF STONE

The history of religion is filled with sacred stones. Prehistoric cultures around the world erected rock monuments, from England's Stonehenge and Ireland's Newgrange to the massive stone heads on Easter Island. Contemporary faiths also recognize sacred stone, including the Dome of the Rock in Jerusalem, which Jews believe is the spot where Abraham prepared to sacrifice his son Isaac and Muslims honor as the place from which Muhammad ascended to heaven. Many Hindu temples have lingam stones representing the god Shiva's generative power, while some Buddhist temples have rock gardens, whose carefully arranged stones and raked sand are designed to aid in meditation. The Ten Commandments were engraved upon stone, and Jesus gave his disciple Simon the new name of Peter (meaning rock) because he would be the foundation of the church.

In nature, our eyes are irresistibly drawn upward by awe-inspiring stone monoliths, including El Capitan in California's Yosemite National Park, Devils Tower in Wyoming, Uluru in Australia, and Sugarloaf Mountain in Rio de Janeiro. Shifting our gaze downward, we marvel at fossils that provide a record of the unfolding of life on earth, from delicate ferns and the graceful coils of ammonoids to the bones of dinosaurs. And what do we do when we reach a natural landmark and want to leave our own mark? We place a rock on a cairn, those piles of rocks that dot many trails, mountaintops, and seashores. Sometimes rocks carry the spirit of a place, in other words, and sometimes they carry our spirit.

One of the most memorable sacred stones I've visited is in Jerusalem's Church of the Holy Sepulchre, the spot where Jesus is said to have been crucified and buried. Just inside the doors of this ancient house of worship is a slab of rock, the Stone of Anointing, which tradition says is where Jesus' body was prepared for burial. I watched as a steady stream of people knelt next to it, some pressing rosaries or crosses against its surface. In a place filled with gilded altars, I found it intriguing that the devotion of pilgrims seemed strongest at this rough-hewn rock.

Stones, it seems, are spiritual paradoxes—inert and yet suffused with energy.

To better understand how rocks can be sacred, I turned to my friend Mary Beth, who is as passionate a lover of stones as anyone I know. When I asked how her love for them had started, she told of growing up near a house with a wall made of stones. Her fascination with the rocks, fossils, and minerals embedded within it are one of her earliest memories.

Then in her forties, she started dreaming about turquoise. "So I went to a rock show, the first one I'd ever visited, and right inside the front door was a table full of turquoise, just like it was waiting for me," she said. "I bought a piece of it, and my connection to stones has gotten stronger ever since."

Mary Beth has even developed a physical response to stones. Usually it's through her left hand, she says, where she feels a slight buzzing when she holds it over particular rocks. Occasionally the attraction is so intense she feels it all through her body. Most of the time she finds her stones on walks, either at home or traveling, though some have been given to her by others and a few purchased.

Because Mary Beth believes that stones are sentient beings, she always asks them if they want to come home with her. "The earth that we live on and the other elements are relatives," she says. "We should be respectful of them."

On a visit to Mary Beth's house, I got the chance to see the rocks she has carefully placed around her yard and house. "They're my prayer partners," she tells me. "When I want to pray for someone, I find a stone from my collection and use it to connect to them. I'll pray over the stone and then put it on my altar. Sometimes if the prayer is answered—if a woman becomes pregnant, for example, or someone's cancer goes into remission—I'll give the stone to them. Other times the stone gets recycled, which means I clear it of energy by pouring water over it or praying over it. Then I put it back into the yard to recharge in the sun."

Mary Beth told a story of the time her husband had a truck-load of river rocks delivered to the new landscaping project in their backyard without telling her about it in advance. The poor man thought he was doing her a favor, but you don't dump a bunch of rocks in a stone lover's yard without asking her first.

"It completely threw me for a loop," recalled Mary Beth. "I sat on our new deck and was thinking about what to do, and suddenly I toppled over backwards. All those new rocks put me off-center."

Once she picked herself up, Mary Beth started working with the new stones, clearing them and inviting them into her home. Then she went around to the stones in her yard, and one by one told them about the new stones. "It turned out OK," she said with a smile. "But I told my husband never to do anything like that again."

Mary Beth's words got me thinking about all the stones Bob has brought home over the years. I don't think he's ever bothered to ask permission before picking one up, and I wondered if any of them are unhappy about being removed from their home.

While I was becoming more attuned to Mary Beth's and Bob's perspectives on stones, I decided it was time to learn some actual science about them. To my surprise I found geology more interesting than I had expected, in part because it's just one cataclysm after another, an epic disaster movie that began when the earth was formed from matter shot into space by the supernova of an exploding star. In our corner of the solar system, those chunks gradually coalesced into a spherical

shape. The mass of the earth began differentiating through
gravitation, heat, and pressure into a thin outer crust, a middle
mantle, and an inner core. Over millions of years continents
formed and re-formed, until the supercontinent of Pangaea
coalesced, only to be broken up by shifting tectonic plates into
the set of continents we have today.

My forays into geology made me realize how wrong I was
in thinking any rock has a permanent home; instead, they're
always on the move, albeit very slowly, even when travelers
don't pick them up and bring them home in their pockets.
Mountains get worn down into valleys, valleys are uplifted
into mountains, tectonic plates shift, lava becomes rock that
becomes sand. My home continent of North America, for
example, has been periodically flooded by tropical seas, blown
apart by volcanoes, torqued by earthquakes, gouged by massive rivers, and scraped by glaciers. Pressure from below forced
up the Rocky Mountains, while the Appalachians were worn
down by weathering. Meteors fell from the sky and sent up
so much debris that it blotted out the sun for years. Studying
geology made me wonder if I should put on a helmet whenever
I went outside.

It all made me think of a story told by my friend Claudia,
who once hosted a visiting geology professor from Cairo for
dinner. When she told him that she thought stones were alive,
he slammed his hand down on the table and told her that she
was the first nongeologist who had ever told him that. "You
get it!" he said.

And now I was starting to get it too.

TEACHERS OF PATIENCE

If stones have a language, I expect it's a very slow language. I
think I've heard murmurs of it at a holy site near my home:
Harvest Preserve, which has a prehistoric sacred stone circle
brought from Indonesia. The tall stones seem surprisingly at
home in Iowa, emerging out of a grassy meadow like they've

been there for millennia. Ancient lichen etches their surfaces, creating patterns that look like abstract paintings. Their tenure in Iowa must seem like the briefest of blips to them, the geologic equivalent of the blink of an eye. On my walks among them I imagine what they are saying to me, which is usually some variation of "Be patient" and "Slow down." They're not chatty, these stones, but they're wise.

My dog Cody seems to get a different message at the standing stones. Typically sedate, when he approaches them he often starts to run in crazy circles, as if he's picking up so much energy from them that he simply has to move. I watch him with amusement and no small amount of envy, wishing I was as attuned as he is.

Cody's reactions to the stones make me think of the New Age capital of Sedona, Arizona, which I visited several years before the pandemic began. At its visitor center I picked up brochures advertising psychic readings, aura photos, past-life regressions, energy vortexes, and UFO-sighting tours. Even the lawyers here advertise their psychic abilities. As I toured its downtown, I loved eavesdropping. ("We're out of fairy dust and unicorn tears," said one clerk to another as I entered a store.) I was especially intrigued by all the crystals, minerals, and stones for sale. Which to choose? They all seemed useful. Amethyst is said to create a bubble of spiritual protection against negative energy; fluorite clears mental clutter; rhodochrosite can heal the past; obsidian activates the root chakra and strengthens your connection to the earth. Their powers might be overrated, but spending five dollars on a rock was certainly cheaper than therapy.

Looking back on that visit after visiting Pipestone, I realized that Sedona's excesses aren't that surprising given the landscape that surrounds it, which is as inherently spiritual as any I've experienced. The town sits in the heart of Red Rock Country, a region that includes the parts of Colorado, Utah, New Mexico, and Arizona where red sandstone predominates. Easily erodible by wind and rain, the region has been shaped over millions of years into canyons, buttes, and sinuously shaped formations such as hoodoos, arches, natural bridges, and arroyos. Rich hues of red, pink, and orange—the colors of pipestone—are splashed across millions of acres. The sunlight plays with the peaks and canyons, lighting up one portion of the landscape after another as the day progresses. In the evening, all you want to do is just sit in a chair and gaze at the rocks, enraptured.

But even ordinary stones, not just showy extroverts like red sandstone, have lessons to teach us. They may not be the philosopher's stone, the magical substance that medieval alchemists thought could turn base metals into gold, but they contain treasures nonetheless. Perhaps their greatest gift to us is a lesson in how to view time. When we hold a stone in our hand, we know it's been in existence for millions—sometimes billions—of years, a thought that can put our troubles into perspective.

Many people also carry stones in their pockets, as Bob has done for decades. This is likely one of the oldest spiritual practices, discovered by many cultures independently. Before there were therapists or therapeutic drugs or self-help books, people found comfort in carrying a smooth stone. Whether they're called worry stones or prayer beads, their function is the same: rubbing them is soothing. In Eastern thought, it's also believed that doing so puts pressure on meridian points on our fingers, activating a flow of energy. A bonus is that no one needs to know when we reach for that little stone, our invisible spiritual companion.

During all my ponderings about rocks, I kept coming back to my time at Pipestone. I remembered the people working in the quarries, using pickaxes and hammers to crack through the quartzite to get to the sacred stone. Oh yeah, that's what the spiritual path is like, I thought. For every brief mountaintop epiphany, you have to put in years of labor in the quarries, digging first through dirt, then using a sledgehammer on rock, all in the quest for the holy. If the Ohio mounds taught me that God might be a mathematician, Pipestone suggests that he might have more in common with an old-school geology professor who demands an insane amount of work for each class.

In my spiritual life, I've felt many times like I needed a pickax to get down to what is important. It especially seemed like this during the pandemic, when a layer of fear and anxiety formed a crust over my heart. It made me think, too, of the sanding and polishing that needs to be done to complete the sacred pipes. I realized that my own rough edges had been polished by difficulties through the years. The reason why river stones are so beautiful and smooth, after all, is because they've been beaten up for centuries.

Is it worth it? All that effort to pry pipestone from the earth and then craft it into a small container, just so smoke can waft its way upward to the Great Spirit? And all that effort to lead a life of the spirit, to pray and meditate and ponder, to try to find ways to serve, all the time plagued by doubts? Whether you're digging for pipestone or trying to follow a spiritual path, in other words, be prepared for a lot of hard work.

As for me, my foray among sacred stones led me to put some of them on my home altar and another one in my pocket. Each rock represents a prayer intention—healing for this person, guidance on a project, a general bless-everyone-and-everything stone, just to make sure all my bases are covered. Some days I think of them as a little silly, but most of the time they are a comfort. Even when I don't have the time or inclination to pray, it feels like they're praying for me, all the while giving me a silent, steady lesson in resilience and patience.

Redwood National and State Parks in California are home to the tallest trees on the planet. (Photo credit: Bob Sessions)

5

Trees: Redwood National and State Parks in California

Because the pandemic didn't have enough angst in it, two weeks after our visit to Pipestone National Monument, my home state of Iowa was hit by one of the worst natural disasters in its history—a windstorm that killed four people, damaged or destroyed more than eight thousand homes, and flattened fourteen million acres of crops. The storm was a *derecho*, a Spanish word meaning "straight," so named because in contrast to a tornado or hurricane that has circular winds, a derecho has straight-line winds that blow through like a freight train.

"Nature is trying to kill us," I told Bob. "First COVID, now this."

Bob and I were away from home when the storm happened, having continued our camping trip after our visit to Pipestone. Out of cell phone range high in the Bighorn Mountains of Wyoming, we didn't hear about the derecho until late the next day.

"It's bad," said the friend who was watching over our house in our absence. "The power is out, and it could be weeks before it comes back on. Luckily your house is OK—just some big branches down in your yard."

We started the two-day drive back the next morning, cutting short our trip because we hoped to empty our refrigerator and freezer before spoiled food made them unusable. About a hundred miles away from home, our hearts sank as we started to see uprooted trees and leveled cornfields. Cedar Rapids—the midwestern city most affected by the storm—was especially distressing to see. Hundreds of damaged houses, some with their roofs torn completely off, were visible from the highway, plus block after block of trees ripped out by their roots and huge branches littering the ground.

Shaken by what we'd seen, when we pulled into our driveway we were filled with relief as we saw our intact house. Some spoiled food in our refrigerator and freezer seemed like a very small thing.

Seeing the uprooted trees of Cedar Rapids was deeply unsettling, an emotion seemingly out of proportion to the damage. They were just trees, after all. The city would plant new ones, and eventually the canopy of green along its streets would be restored.

But it still felt as if something sacred had been violated. My reaction made me realize the depth of the lifelong bond I've had with trees, beginning in my childhood when our farm's woods were my primary playground, a place to build forts, stage dramas, and perch on a branch to see the world passing by below. That love continued into adulthood, when forests became less about play and more about appreciating their ever-changing beauty. (No disrespect to evergreens, but the oaks, maples, hickories, and walnut trees of Iowa first won my heart.) In spring, I love how delicate new leaves throw a tracery of yellowish-green over the hills, and in summer how Iowa's heat is tempered by those same leaves, now thick and abundant. Autumn is the time for deciduous trees to show off, a weeks-long competition to see who can blaze most brightly with crimson, orange, yellow, and scarlet, but I like the trees of winter nearly as much, especially on evenings when multicolored sunsets glow behind bare branches so that the horizon looks like it's framed by stained glass windows.

I can also thank my ancestors—my very *distant* ancestors— for my reaction to the damaged and uprooted trees in Cedar Rapids. Early hominids in Africa lived in trees, and even after they took up residence on the ground they likely still returned to the safety of their former homes in times of danger. If you've ever felt exposed and vulnerable in an open landscape without trees, you know how our ancestors felt in similar situations. Our evolution into modern humans continued to be tied to trees as we learned by trial and error the many uses of wood, from cooking and heating to building tools, houses, wagons, and boats. For the vast majority of our history, wood was the single most useful material we possessed. "Wood once constituted the greatest part of the wealth of tribes and of nations," writes William Bryant Logan in *Oak: The Frame of Civilization*. "Since the glaciers last retreated and since humans began to build and settle down, there have been but two versions of the world: the world made with wood and the world made with coal and oil. One lasted twelve to fifteen millennia; the other has lasted about 250 years so far . . . [though] these later fuels, indeed, embody no new principle. They are just old stem and branch and leaf and root, entombed for eons and distilled, the remnants of a wooden world from before the coming of humankind."

Through the millennia we've learned that trees are great teachers if we just slow down and observe them. They're marvelously resilient and can survive fire, floods, and storms (during which their capacity to bend, rather than break, gives us a lesson in how to weather a crisis). They're extravagantly lush, with many species creating hundreds of thousands of leaves each season only to lose them each fall, an annual demonstration of the need to let go in order to thrive. They're determined to reproduce against astronomical odds, flinging their seeds into the wind like profligate spenders who can't be bothered to keep to a budget. A single maple in a forest can produce tens of thousands of seeds a year, of which only a few might grow to maturity. The root system of trees reminds us that if we want to grow tall it's best to burrow deep, while the way in which deciduous trees slumber through winter and are reborn each spring makes them living exemplars of resurrection.

Given how closely our evolution is tied to trees, it's not surprising they feature prominently in the world's religions. The Bible begins with the story of the Tree of the Knowledge of Good and Evil, whose oh-so-tempting fruit got Adam and Eve kicked out of paradise, and ends with a scene at the Tree of Life in the book of Revelation. The prophet Jeremiah has a beautiful passage about trees in which he says:

> Blessed are those who trust in the LORD,
>   whose trust is the LORD.
> They shall be like a tree planted by water,
>   sending out its roots by the stream.
> It shall not fear when heat comes,
>   and its leaves shall stay green;
> in the year of drought it is not anxious,
>   and it does not cease to bear fruit.
>   (Jeremiah 17:7–8)

The cross on which Jesus died was made of wood, and a tree has at times been used interchangeably with the cross as a symbol (in early medieval manuscripts, the cross was sometimes depicted with the sawn-off nubs of branches). In the Kabbalah—the mystical tradition of Judaism—the Tree of Life is the primary symbol for the ineffable aspects of the Creator. In Hinduism, certain tree species are associated with deities, including the neem tree's tie to the goddess Durga and the god Krishna's association with the kadamba tree. In Buddhism, the most significant events in the life of the Buddha are associated with trees, from his birth under a shala tree and enlightenment under a bodhi tree to his death beneath two shalas. In Japan, cherry trees are beloved because their blossoms provide a powerful teaching on the ephemeral nature of life, while in many African cultures the baobab tree is celebrated in legends and stories.

In ancient Greece, female spirits known as dryads were associated with trees, including several who were turned into *actual* trees in order to escape the lustful advances of the gods. The resemblance between trees and humans is obvious even in those who haven't been transmogrified in this way. We too have slender columns for bodies and long arms that wave in the air, plus blood that's similar to sap (though our toes are planted on—rather than in—the ground). Perhaps this is one of the reasons why around the world one of the most common ways to honor a loved one is to plant a tree in their memory.

Few groups revered trees as much as the Celtic Druids of the pre-Christian British Isles. *Druid* itself is derived from words meaning "knower of oaks," and these lawgivers and bards worshiped in sacred oak groves, ate acorns in hopes of having prophetic visions, and honored the mistletoe, a parasitic species common in oaks. The Christmas tradition of kissing under a mistletoe likely dates back to their respect for the plant.

The life of St. Columba, one of the patron saints of Ireland, shows that this respect continued into the Christian era. Columba may have been a Druid before his conversion, a theory supported by his lifelong reverence for trees. He told his followers not to touch any fallen tree for nine days (nine was a sacred number for the pagan Celts), and when he founded a monastery at Derry in 546 he built his oratory facing north-south, instead of the traditional east-west, because he didn't want to disturb the surrounding trees. He said that while he feared death and the fires of hell, he feared the sound of an axe in Derry even more.

PRIMEVAL FOREST

The sacredness of trees came to my mind one frigid January day as I was contemplating time's winged chariot drawing near in the form of my upcoming sixtieth birthday. Entering a new decade merited something special, I thought, which made me think of a landscape I'd long dreamed of visiting: the redwoods of California. It would be reassuring to spend time among creatures much older than I was, for one thing, and surely a book on sacred landscapes needed to include the most remarkable forests in North America.

I searched for "best place to camp under the redwoods," and on the many websites that popped up, Jedediah Smith Redwoods State Park was mentioned again and again. I pulled up a digital map and did the driving math: 2,080 miles, or 30 hours and 10 minutes, assuming we never took a bathroom break or slept. "Do you want to go to the redwoods for my birthday?" I called downstairs to Bob. "They're only 2,000 miles away."

Because Bob is basically a Druid, I knew that the prospect of a long road trip wouldn't faze him if huge trees were waiting at the end of it. Sure enough: "Do we have to wait until May to go?" he called back up the stairs. With a smile, I leaned back in my chair and looked out my office window at a barren landscape of snow, ice, and bare trees, already dreaming of a landscape of forest giants amid lush greenery.

As I planned our trip, I learned about the three subspecies of redwoods. Giant sequoias grow on the western slopes of California's Sierra Nevada Mountains and are the largest trees by volume in the world. Dawn redwoods, the stature-challenged underachievers of the redwood clan, were thought to be extinct before being rediscovered in China in 1944 and are now often planted as ornamental trees in gardens. But the true giants are the coast redwoods (*Sequoia sempervirens*), which grow only in northern California and the southwestern tip of Oregon. The coast redwoods have been compared to shy cats, though cats that are up to 380 feet tall. They need to be near the coast so they can absorb water from the frequent fogs that roll in from the ocean, but because they don't like the salt air they congregate in valleys that block the sea winds. That, combined with the fact that for many years their lumber was harvested without restrictions, means that just 4 percent of old-growth redwoods remain.

Jedediah Smith Redwoods State Park seemed like an ideal base for exploring this landscape. It's the northernmost of a

patchwork of redwood parks jointly managed by the California State Parks system and the National Park Service. Located
nine miles northeast of Crescent City, Jed Smith (as it's affec-
tionately known by its fans) has some of the densest temperate
rainforest on earth. Named after an early white explorer to the
region, it's bisected by the Smith River, the longest major free-
flowing river in California. Browsing its website, I was pleased
to learn that its 10,000 acres contain some of the world's oldest
and tallest redwoods—perfect companions for celebrating my
decade birthday.

We left home in mid-May, towing our little teardrop camper
that would be our home for a month. We traveled through
Iowa, Nebraska, Wyoming, Utah, Idaho, and Oregon, an
epic road trip that gave me plenty of time to contemplate my
upcoming birthday. The trees began to take on a mystical stature in my mind, gurus of wood who might be able to teach me
the secret of growing old gracefully.

Once we crossed the border into California, the forests
grew thicker, more luxuriant, and taller. Road weary, at last we
turned into Jedediah Smith Redwoods State Park and within
a half mile saw the object of our quest: the coast redwoods,
which stretched tall and straight in the forest all around us,
their tops hidden by the roof of the car. Between Bob's Dru-
idness and my own musings on the redwoods as the perfect
place to enter a new stage of life, it felt like we'd reached the
promised land.

I remember that first evening among the redwoods as one
of the most magical times of my life. The slanting light of the
fading day sent shafts of light among the trees, illuminating
patches of huge ferns on the forest floor and giving the entire
scene a Garden of Eden vibe. After setting up camp, we went
for a walk along a nearby nature trail, stopping every few yards
to crane our necks and look upward, exclaiming in wonder all
the while. "Look at that one!" "Amazing!" "That one's even
bigger!" But gradually we stopped talking, because after a while
we remembered, as we had in many holy places around the
world, that silence is often the best way to honor the sacred.

I tried to imagine the trees wishing me a happy birthday, but the thought seemed ridiculous. These beings had other, much deeper, things on their minds.

THE AXIS OF THE WORLD

Being among the redwoods gave me fresh insight into the ancient concept of the World Tree, an idea common in cultures from Siberia and China to India and Mexico. While the details vary, the central concept is that an *axis mundi*, or world axis, unites heaven, earth, and the underworld, creating a circuit of energy that makes it possible to communicate and travel between the different realms.

One of the most famous of the World Trees is Yggdrasil, a giant tree in Norse mythology that links the nine worlds of the cosmos. Tended by supernatural beings known as the Norns and watered by a well of wisdom at its roots, its health is essential for the continuation of the universe. During the pagan era, many Scandinavian farms had their own version of Yggdrasil, a tree that was believed to connect to a sacred source. Known in Norwegian as a *tuntre*, the tree was never to be cut down or damaged because it protected the land and its inhabitants. (A variation of this tradition continues in Scandinavia to this day, long after the Norse gods have departed.) And just as the mistletoe tradition can be traced to the pre-Christian past of England, the practice of bringing an evergreen into our homes at Christmas carries an echo of the pagan belief in the sacredness of trees, especially the evergreens that remain miraculously green during winter.

My time in the redwoods brought back another experience I'd had with huge trees—and maybe with the World Tree itself, or at least one of its emissaries. Several years ago Bob and I were in New Zealand on a Maori heritage and culture tour that took us to a variety of sites on the North Island. Near the end of our trip we traveled to the Waipoua Forest, an ecological treasure that includes old-growth kauri trees that were never logged because of their inaccessibility. The kauri, a species that dates back to the Jurassic Period, are among the oldest, largest, and longest-lived of all tree species. When Europeans came to New Zealand in the eighteenth century, they began harvesting these magnificent trees, which were valuable because of both their durable wood and their resin, which has many industrial uses. The giants were felled, one by one, and much of the lumber was shipped across the sea. By the time the government passed laws protecting the remaining forests, just 4 percent of their original range remained.

Our Maori guides met us at the edge of Waipoua Forest. Before we began our hike, they said a prayer in Maori, asking for our protection as we walked. Though I didn't understand the language, the ritual was familiar: before you enter a holy place, you prepare yourself. After finishing their prayer, one of the guides explained that while all kauri trees are sacred to the Maori, they have special reverence for Te Matua Ngahere, the Father of the Forest, who is among the oldest of all the remaining kauri trees. Then we started off on a path that led to this giant, winding our way through underbrush thick with ferns, shrubs, mosses, lichens, epiphytes, and trees such as tawa and taraire.

As we walked, our guides pointed out the occasional kauri trees that we passed, each one larger than the last. "That one is a baby, just eight hundred years old," they said of one. "This one is a thousand years, still pretty young," they said about another.

On our walk the guides told a Maori story about how the whales once asked the kauri to live in the ocean with them as brothers. The trees refused but agreed to swap skins, which is why they have such thin bark. They also explained that the Maori honor these trees as sacred kin because they believe an ancestor of the kauri tree created life. "When Sky Father and Mother Earth were locked in a passionate embrace, it was the kauri tree that separated them, creating space for light," explained one of the men.

After a half hour of walking we came to a ravine where we could see a glimmer of a huge trunk ahead of us, its whiteness glowing in the fading light of evening. The guide walking behind us began to sing to the tree in Maori, a song picked up by the other guide at the front of our group. As we approached Te Matua Ngahere, their song of greeting and praise made us instinctively slow our steps in a sign of reverence. At last we arrived at its base and gazed upward in awe at the sight before us: a tree a hundred feet tall, its trunk so massive that it made the surrounding trees look like matchsticks. I knew from our guides that this tree might well have been a seedling when Jesus was born. Growing only a millimeter or so each year, it had slowly inched its way up over many centuries, forming a crown held aloft by a ramrod-straight trunk whose branches start thirty-five feet above the earth.

Our group stood looking upward in silence, the same hush that had fallen upon Bob and me in the redwoods. There was no doubt this was indeed the Father of the Forest and that we were standing on holy ground. I blinked rapidly, surprised at the tears that had come to my eyes, to me a sure sign of being in the presence of the sacred.

TRACING THE WOOD-WIDE WEB

In some ways it's unfortunate to use sylvan superstars like the kauri and redwoods as examples of sacred wood, which is like saying that Notre Dame Cathedral in Paris is the only church worth visiting. In reality, even seemingly ordinary trees are wondrous. They clean the air, filter water, stabilize soil, nurture biodiversity, sequester carbon, and provide us with useful products, from wood and nuts to turpentine. They're skilled historians, recording in their trunks a record of the growing conditions they've experienced each year. And they're good neighbors too, except for the occasional branch or trunk that lands on our roof. Shaded homes are up to 10 degrees cooler than ones in full sun, and houses with trees tend to have higher property values.

Within the past decade, researchers have learned an additional remarkable characteristic of trees: they benefit from hanging out together, like teenagers at a mall or cousins at a family reunion. Underneath the ground, an intricate network of soil fungi allows trees to communicate, share nutrients, and nurture the young and weak, a process discovered by Suzanne Simard, a forest ecology researcher in British Columbia. In describing her initial understanding of how trees are connected underneath the ground, she writes,

> This forest was like the Internet—the World Wide Web. But instead of computers linked by wires or radio waves, these trees were connected by mycorrhizal fungi. The forest seemed like a system of centers and satellites, where the old trees were the biggest communication hubs and the smaller ones the less-busy nodes, with messages transmitting back and forth through the fungal links. Back in 1997 when my article had been published in *Nature*, the journal had called it the "wood-wide web," and that was turning out to be much more prescient than I'd imagined.

In the early years of Simard's research on forests, she was careful not to extrapolate too far from her data. But when she realized that traditional scientific language couldn't capture the complexities of what she was discovering, she began using phrases such as *mother trees* and *forest wisdom* to convey the surprising ways forests have a kind of agency and even consciousness. "There's so much more going on in forests than we're able to actually understand using the traditional scientific techniques," she said in an interview with *Yale Environment 360*, "So I opened my mind up and said we need to bring in human aspects to this so that we understand deeper, more viscerally, what's going on in these living creatures, species that are not just these inanimate objects. . . . To me, using the language of communication made more sense because we were looking not just at resource transfers, but things like defense signaling and kin recognition signaling." In other words, forests and human communities have a lot in common, which is a spiritual insight that goes back millennia.

Another time-honored insight that science has corroborated is that it simply makes us feel *better* to be around trees. No nation has put more effort into figuring out why this is so than Japan, which has a long tradition of honoring forests. Its indigenous Shinto religion believes forests are the dwelling places of the gods, and countless Buddhist practitioners have sought inspiration in the woods. Today the country is home to the International Society of Nature and Forest Medicine, which studies the health benefits of relaxing in forests. Studies done by its members have shown that a walk in the forest can reduce levels of stress hormones, lower blood pressure, and increase the number of natural killer (NK) cells that fight tumors and viruses. These benefits are likely tied in part to phytoncides, which are antimicrobial volatile organic compounds derived from plants. (Think of the slightly citrusy smell of pines or the woody aromas of oaks.) The fresh scents that bathe our sinuses on a walk through the woods come from compounds produced by the trees to protect themselves from harmful insects and diseases. When we breathe them in, we benefit too.

The Japanese term for seeking healing in nature is *shinrin-yoku*, which is translated as "forest bathing." (Despite the name, alas, most practitioners keep their clothes on.) What makes forest bathing different from an ordinary stroll through the woods is how deliberate and mindful it is. Instead of just walking under the trees, you're sniffing, touching, and feeling the wind on your face. You might nibble on a leaf or stretch out on a sun-warmed boulder. Think of it as the perfect excuse to act like a stoned hippie staring at tree bark and saying "Wow!" over and over.

While forest bathing classes are held around the United States, I decided to do my own freelance *shinrin-yoku*. On my walks through local parks I tried to practice the technique, slowing my usual walking pace and gazing intently at the trees around me. I took deep breaths, feeling those helpful phytoncides filling my lungs, and—in an effort to blend science with spirituality—imagined wood nymphs peeking out from behind the trunks. I speculated on their personalities, wondering if they spoke in a raspy burr-oak sort of way or with an aspen's rustling whisper. Whatever their voices sounded like, I bet they talked a lot about the weather, even more so than most midwesterners.

My forest bathing experiences were fun but not, I must admit, especially enlightening. That's when I decided to buy a hammock, one in a trunk-friendly design that I set up between two trees in our backyard. Stretched out in its embrace, I spent relaxing afternoons trying to deepen my understanding of sacred wood ("I can't mow the lawn, Bob—can't you see I'm working?"). Easily packed and simple to set up, my hammock became a necessity on camping trips. I relished the different perspectives it gave me as I gazed upward at skies filtered by leaves and branches. Even on a calm day I could sense the slight movements of the trees holding me up, as if they were gently rocking me back and forth in the instinctive action of mothers. Suzanne Simard is right: there are indeed mother trees.

FOREST KIN

During our week among the redwoods, I thought about another familial metaphor relating to trees, the Maori story about how the kauri trees and whales are brothers. Redwoods must be part of that same clan, I reasoned, though their bark is much thicker than that of the kauri. Growing from a seed no bigger than that of a tomato, redwoods are the terrestrial equivalent of blue whales, the largest animal the earth has ever produced. Reaching heights that can rival those of a thirty-story skyscraper, they're extremely resistant to fire, insects, and disease and can reach an age of more than two millennia, which makes them among the oldest living organisms in the world. Having appeared as a species shortly after the dinosaurs disappeared, they give us glimpses of what the world was like eons ago.

Humans have been hard on both redwoods and whales. The massive trees once covered more than two million acres in California, but commercial logging of the highly prized wood has claimed more than 95 percent of the virgin forests. The nonprofit Save the Redwoods League, founded in 1918, was one of a broad coalition of groups and individuals that have worked to protect the remaining forests. Thanks in large part to their efforts, the state redwoods parks were created, followed by the establishment of Redwood National Park in 1968. Together, the national park and three state parks protect 133,000 acres of coast redwoods and are replanting and restoring the logged areas.

While the regrowth initiatives are laudable, as Bob and I hiked we could see the dramatic differences between old-growth and secondary-growth forests. The old giants have a stature and presence that's fundamentally different from the younger trees. The ents from *The Lord of the Rings*—that race of tree-beings who look with bemusement at the hobbits who insist on doing everything quickly—came to my mind as we walked among them. That's what we must seem like to these trees, I thought, so intent on racing through life, so unwilling to settle down and just be. I speculated, too, on the possible appearance of redwood nymphs, imagining them as stout giantesses with tangled red hair and mossy teeth.

In Northern California many of the oldest ents—er, trees—grow in groups known as groves. Some of the most beautiful have been given names, including Stout Grove in Jedediah Smith State Park and the Lady Bird Johnson Grove in Redwood National Park, which honors the former first lady who had a passion for conservation. The trees cluster in this way because seedlings often germinate from the roots of parent trees. As they grow, their roots intertwine with older trees, giving all of them extra stability in wind and storms. That's a key part of their survival, because while redwood roots can extend eighty feet from the trunk horizontally, they're just six to twelve feet deep.

The redwoods live in a moist, cool world, with sixty to eighty inches of rain a year and temperatures typically ranging between forty and sixty degrees. Just off the public walkways the forest floor is a tangled mass of smallish trees, bushes, and ferns, making it impenetrable for all but the most determined explorers. This is among the most biologically diverse biomes in the world, rivaling even the Amazon.

On our hikes, I was struck by the hush that prevails in many of these redwood forests. It seemed to come not only from our own silence but from a deep stillness within the forest itself. It's not surprising these redwood groves are frequently compared to cathedrals, only instead of pillars of stone they have pillars of trees, so tall that their tops are hidden from view. It made me wonder whether the medieval builders of cathedrals honored their ancestral bond with the great forests of Europe by modeling their churches on them. In his classic study of comparative religion, *The Golden Bough: A Study in Magic and Religion*, Sir James George Frazer writes,

> For at the dawn of history Europe was covered with immense primaeval forests, in which the scattered clearings must have appeared like islets in an ocean of green. Down to the first century before our era . . . [the] forest stretched eastward from the Rhine for a distance at once vast and unknown; Germans whom Caesar questioned had travelled for two months through it without reaching the end. Four centuries later it was visited by the Emperor Julian, and the solitude, the gloom, the silence of the forest appear to have made a deep impression on his sensitive nature. He declared that he knew nothing like it in the Roman empire.

I thought of the Maori, singing to the Father of the Forest, and wished I had my own song to sing to the redwoods.

My favorite times in the redwoods were the mornings when fog from the ocean wreathed the tall columns of the trees. The forest looked otherworldly, as if a powerful magician had flung an enchantment over the landscape. I wandered among the mist-swirled trees, thinking not just of the redwoods but of all the trees I've loved in my life—those oaks, pines, hickories, and willows that have lifted my heart and calmed my spirit. One is the maple in our front yard, which Bob and I planted a dozen years ago and which I've dubbed a *tuntre*, our link to Yggdrasil, the World Tree. I've cheered its growth ever since, watching the slow unfurling of its branches and widening of its trunk. I hope the tree will continue to protect those who live in our house after us, even though they won't know its secret identity.

As I walked beneath the redwoods on our last day, I thought as well about the lessons I'd learned from my time among these forest giants. While it may seem like hubris to expect a birthday gift from them, I've long believed that travelers with open hearts receive blessings on their pilgrimages. So what teaching would I take with me when Bob and I left the redwoods the next morning? Perhaps that I shouldn't be afraid of fire. Or in my case, I shouldn't be afraid of the troubles, trials, and inevitable indignities of aging. That message came from seeing all the fire-ravaged elders of the forest, the ones that had been damaged by long-ago infernos. They'd slowly recovered, growing new bark around the edges of their injuries, but their scars would always remain. I felt a rush of affection for these gnarled beings, some of whom had been so hollowed out by fire that it wasn't clear how they could remain standing. They reminded me that among the elders of all species, it's a rare being who doesn't bear the marks of long-ago traumas. They prove to us that true beauty lies not in perfection, but in endurance.

I have some scars myself, thanks to my sixty years, and I know that eventually I'll topple over in some big storm, just like these redwoods will. But for now we both are determined to grow upward in search of the light, as tall and straight as we can manage, glorying in sacred flesh and sacred wood.

In the Cascade Mountains of Oregon, a remote hot spring attracts water-loving pilgrims. (Photo credit: Bob Sessions)

6

Water: The Hot Springs of Oregon

One morning early in the pandemic I opened up an email with devastating news. Shaken, I headed downstairs to the living room where Bob was reading a book.

"What's wrong?" he asked with concern, seeing my stricken look.

"The swimming pool is closing because of COVID," I said.

"Well, that's too bad," Bob said, and went back to his book.

His response made me realize once again the trials of having a mixed marriage. While I'm a water person, Bob is a trees-and-mountains guy who gets bored after a half hour sitting on a beach. As I'm sitting enthralled by the rhythmic waves, he's complaining about the heat and strategizing about where we can find a place to hike. No wonder he didn't appreciate the depth of my anguish when my favorite exercise was being taken from me. Though I'm not an adept swimmer, I visited the local indoor pool several times a week, reveling in the medita-tive, repetitive movements of swimming and the sense of free-dom the water gave me. Swimming in a nearby lake wasn't an option, given the cold weather, and even in the warm months

I'm not confident in open water, so that email I'd clicked open was bad news indeed.

"It's not just *too bad*—it's a disaster," I corrected Bob, so overwhelmed by gloom that I failed to realize that not being able to go swimming was pretty far down on the list of terrible things about the pandemic.

The months passed, and I coped without my swimming routine, but my time away from the water made me love it all the more. I thought longingly about what I was missing, remembering the silky feel of the water and how swimming creates a cocoon in which the outside world recedes and no one can bother you. I sometimes pretended I was flying in the water, swimming under the surface with breaststrokes that I imagined were the smooth glide of wings. Even if my skill level was amateurish next to the more experienced swimmers in neighboring lanes, it didn't matter if I was a tadpole and they were dolphins. Soothed by the steady rhythm of my strokes, I worked out problems, daydreamed, and simply breathed—a kind of meditation-for-dummies thanks to the quiet rhythm of my strokes in the pool.

So once we started on our expeditions across America in search of holy places, I snuck in as many lakes, rivers, and other bodies of water as I could. Shamelessly taking advantage of the need to do research, I tricked Bob into more water experiences than he'd had during our entire marriage. We kayaked, walked along rivers, took boat rides, and sat on beaches, me enraptured and Bob making the best of it. And once we left the California redwoods, I rejoiced that even more water experiences awaited us in Oregon. Bordered by the Pacific Ocean, laced with rivers and streams, and bubbling with hot springs, the state is a prime destination for swimmers, soakers, paddlers, sailors, and waders—and for me, an aspiring water nymph.

JUST ADD WATER

If I had to tally the number of fans of the various sacred elements I've been chronicling, I would guess that water has more devotees than anything else. Our distant ancestors crawled out of it billions of years ago, and many of us have been wanting to dive back in ever since.

We have plenty of options when we start exploring water, because more than 70 percent of the earth's surface is covered with it. Viewed from space, the earth is a blue marble. (As author Arthur C. Clarke noted, it's inappropriate to call this planet Earth when it's quite clearly Ocean.) The combination of two hydrogen atoms and one oxygen atom is responsible for a dazzling range of landscapes and weather phenomena, from the sculpted glaciers of the polar regions and the billowing clouds of thunderstorms to the gushing waterfalls of rainforests.

Humans spend their first nine months as water beings, floating in amniotic fluid whose salt level is just a little less than that of the ocean. Once we're born, our bodies are mostly water, too, with the average adult made up of about 60 percent water, while infants are about 75 percent (not surprising to anyone who's had to clean up the many forms of fluid expelled from them). Some parts of our body are more saturated than others: our lungs are approximately 83 percent; kidneys 79 percent; and heart and brain 73 percent. We start to feel thirsty when we've lost just 2 percent of our water, and even being mildly dehydrated can impair our cognitive and physical performance.

Not everyone loves being around water, just as not everyone loves a walk in a forest. But for the majority of people, simply being around water makes them feel good. That helps explain why about 40 percent of the world's population lives within sixty miles of a coastline and why even a shack with an ocean view can be outrageously expensive.

Marine biologist Wallace J. Nichols explores the many reasons why water is good for us in his book *Blue Mind: The Surprising Science That Shows How Being Near, In, On, or Under Water Can Make You Happier, Healthier, More Connected, and Better at What You Do*. Nichols defines "Blue Mind" as a mildly meditative state characterized by calm, peacefulness, unity, and a sense of general happiness and satisfaction with life in the moment. His book is full of examples of its effects. Writes Nichols,

> From the early Greek and Roman physicians who recognized the healing waters of nature and bathing; to stressed-out industrial workers in nineteenth-century England and the United States who were advised to "take the waters" by the seaside or at natural springs to recover; to men and women today who treat their drug and alcohol addictions or PTSD with the dopamine rush of surfing or with the endorphin serenity produced by long, calm hours with a fishing rod in their hands; to patients who stare at aquariums in dental waiting rooms and feel reduced anxiety after watching the fish; to the millions who step into a hot bath or shower at the end of a long day and emerge relaxed, refreshed, and renewed—all of these are examples of how water can help us transition from the Red Mind of stress or the Gray Mind of numbed-out depression to the healthier Blue Mind state of calm centeredness.

Part of water's magnetism is simply that it's beautiful. Lakes, ponds, and seas are mirrors that reflect and refract light, creating patterns that are both constantly changing and soothingly similar. That's why many of us can watch waves for hours and not be bored, as our brains are lulled into a state of rest and our neural pathways cleared for inspiration and healing. Add to that the sounds of water, from rain on the roof to the steady pulse of waves, and you have a formula for relaxation and rejuvenation.

I realize it's easy to get all misty-eyed about the wonders of water until you have to deal with too much of it in the wrong place. Water also has negative aspects, including floods, hurricanes, severe thunderstorms, rip tides, and drownings, plus the fetid indignity of sewage backup in basements. That's why mythologies around the world have stories about the dangers of water, from the sea god Poseidon demanding human sacrifices and the Sirens luring sailors to wreck their ships, to the water nymphs who fiercely guard springs and rivers. Like all spiritual elements water has a shadow side, made all the more dangerous by how appealing it can look on the surface. Maybe more than any other element, it both gives life and takes it away. And while we know in our minds its dangers, like sailors tricked by the Sirens our hearts are still entranced by the call of the sea.

MAGICAL SPRINGS

As a land-locked Iowan I've long loved the sea with the passion of someone who sees her beloved only rarely, so the week Bob and I spent along the Oregon coast was heaven. We camped in the state parks that line its length, hiked its windswept head-lands, and spent hours on its gray-sand beaches. Though the water was too cold to even wade in comfortably, the sounds, smells, and sights of the ocean nurtured the deepest nooks and crannies of my soul.

But the real goal of our time in the state was to explore its hot springs, which are a form of water I'd rarely experienced. A precise set of conditions is needed to create hot springs, which typically form in areas with either active or dormant volcanoes. Magma beneath the surface heats groundwater, which rises upward through cracks and fissures in the earth. In the United States the majority of hot springs are in the West because the Rockies are a young mountain range with a lot of geothermal heat beneath them. Oregon in particular has some of the best hot springs in the nation because it's located on a chain of mostly dormant volcanoes. While a handful of its springs have been commercially developed, many are known mostly through word of mouth, though with the internet it's harder for locals to keep their private Shangri-La a secret. Some are located in remote sites on national forest land so that you either have to stumble upon them or be told their whereabouts by a resident. In keeping with that ethic, I'll keep mum about the location of two of the isolated springs we visited, because much of what makes these small springs attractive is that not many people visit them.

As I planned our trip inland from the Oregon coast I scoured websites, blogs, and guidebooks for information, designing a route to visit as many hot springs as I could find. "That's sure a lot of hot springs," Bob said when I showed him our itinerary. "You will love them!" I assured him.

Bob sighed, determined to make the best of it but clearly not entirely enthusiastic. I understood his hesitation, because in some ways all you have to do for a hot springs experience is go into the privacy of your bathroom, shut the door, and draw a bath, without all the difficulties of trekking through a forest, slipping on rocks, and sharing your soak with total strangers.

So what is so special about a hot spring? Well, let me count the ways. One is that they have *hot water* and they're *outside*. Hot springs remind us that a roiling cauldron of liquified rock exists underneath our feet, proof that the earth is a powerhouse of fiery energy. Plus, as you soak, you're surrounded by the sensual richness of the natural world—trees, birdsong, sunshine, maybe some mountains if you're lucky. When it's cold outside, the temperature just adds to the wonder of the experience, with the water creating great clouds of steam. Hot springs may well have actual medicinal qualities too, thanks to the minerals that many of them contain—often some combination of silica, bicarbonate, magnesium, selenium, potassium, lithium, and iron, each of which is said to have a positive effect on health. Hot springs, in short, are water in its most inviting form, even if some are accompanied by a faint whiff of sulphur.

Our hot springs tour began with a visit to Crane Hot Springs, a commercially developed resort in the high desert of southeastern Oregon. Snow flurries and a stiff north wind made our sprint from the changing rooms to the pool a shivering ordeal, but once we got into the hot water all was forgiven. I floated on my back in the middle of the pool, reveling in the feeling of being cold on one side and hot on the other. "You can't do this in a bathtub," I told Bob, who had to agree.

The next springs were disappointing, however. The first took us ages to find, and when we finally did it was already occupied by a naked, scrawny guy with a gray ponytail, who stood knee-deep in muddy water as he poured water over his head, obviously trying to have a good time despite the limitations of the spring. "Join me!" he called, his face hopeful, but we politely declined. Another spring had a picturesque wooded setting and steaming water, but way too many people were crowded into it, making us hesitant to join them. Yet another we simply couldn't find at all, despite poring over maps. (In the boonies of Oregon, good luck finding an internet connection.)

I was beginning to think maybe I'd oversold the entire hot springs experience to Bob, who had the martyred expression on his face that I recognized from previous wild goose chases. Perhaps I'd oversold it to myself as well, I wondered. Maybe I should be content with sacred waters in the form of oceans, rivers, and streams and not be greedy for more. I looked at my hand-drawn map once again. Two more springs to go. Maybe we'd get lucky.

And we did, though it didn't seem like it at first. We pulled into a parking lot high in the Cascade Mountains and followed a winding path a short way to the site of the springs, which flowed from a small cave in the hillside next to a river. A semi-circle of stones had been piled up to keep the warm water contained. It looked inviting, though once again the spring was occupied, this time by a family of five. "We should leave it to them," Bob said, but I demurred, reminding him that according to hot springs etiquette, as long as there is room in the water everyone is welcome. "You go for a walk," I said. "I'm staying."

I took off the T-shirt and shorts I was wearing over my swimsuit and eased myself into the water, which was the perfect temperature, warm but not too hot. I soon struck up a conversation with my bathing companions, who had moved to Oregon from Tennessee the year before. After living in a camper for several months, they'd purchased land in the middle of an area that had recently been ravaged by a forest fire. "We got it cheap," the dad said proudly. The kids, who were all homeschooled, seemed pleased with their new lives and had an impressive knowledge of the life cycle of the dragonflies that were flitting around us.

After a few minutes, the mother announced it was time to leave. "You've had your bath for the week," she told the children. "We need to leave if we're going to make it home before dark."

After they left, I savored the solitude, knowing it could be broken at any minute by more visitors or Bob returning from his walk. I ventured farther into the cave, the water getting warmer as I went. I found a comfortable place to sit, my body mostly submerged, with drops of cold water falling onto me from the roof a foot above my head. As I looked outside, the mouth of the cave formed a frame for the brilliant colors of the forest and river, the rushing of the water a soothing melody. The water dripping from the roof seemed like a kind of baptism, a confirmation that my sixtieth birthday in the redwoods had indeed launched a new stage in my life. I smiled, sinking down deeper into the water, savoring the sensual pleasures of warmth, the gorgeous view, and the womblike feeling of being enveloped by the small, dark cave.

My utopia in the hot spring lasted for maybe only fifteen minutes, but it was enough to infuse my entire being with contentment. I was so mellow that I didn't even mind when a couple dressed in hiking gear came into view. "Do you mind if we join you?" the young woman asked.

"I'm just leaving," I answered. "It's all yours."

I walked back to the car with a light step, not minding the coolness of the mountain air on my damp skin, watching in wonder as butterflies fluttered on the path ahead of me like sparkling lights from another realm.

YES, WE SHALL GATHER AT THE RIVER

While experiences like this made me an aspiring water nymph, water also made me a Christian. It happened when I was a few weeks old and my parents took me to our small Lutheran church in rural Iowa, where a pastor sprinkled water on my head and welcomed me into the faith. Some denominations practice full immersion baptism, waiting until people are capable of making their own decision to receive the rite. But whenever baptism happens, water is the element that facilitates a sacred transformation.

The practice goes back to Jesus himself, who was baptized in the Jordan River by his cousin John (who performed this ritual so many times that he was known as John the Baptist). A number of years ago I visited the Yardenit Baptismal Site on the Jordan River in Israel, which is a popular spot for visiting pilgrims to be baptized, even though the actual spot for Jesus' baptism was likely farther south, near Jericho. I savored the birdsongs and lush plants growing near the river, an oasis of green in a dry and dusty countryside. Panels near the river were lined with the story of Jesus' baptism in more than sixty languages, and I could hear Russian, Chinese, and several other languages I didn't recognize. I watched as dozens of people, all wearing white clothing, were dipped under the water and then emerged, dripping, into the bright sunlight, some looking self-conscious but others radiant. From Iowa to Israel, baptism is still a powerful ceremony of rebirth.

Jesus said he would give his followers "living water," a statement that theologians are still trying to unpack. He may have been referring to the Holy Spirit or to the promise of eternal life, or maybe he was simply using a metaphor designed to appeal to people living in a parched land. To this day, many Christian denominations add a small amount of water to the Communion cup used during the Eucharist, a symbolic echo of the water that poured from Jesus' side at his crucifixion. Catholic churches have water that's been blessed by a priest at their front doors, which people use to make the sign of the cross on themselves before entering.

Many other religions include water in their rituals, often as a form of ritual cleansing. Judaism has the practice of the mikveh, a pool of water used for purification, including before women are married and after they have menstruated. Hinduism has sacred rivers to which pilgrimages are made, while Muslims do ritual washing before prayers. In Buddhism, one of the most beautiful teachings about water comes from the Vietnamese teacher Thich Nhat Hanh, who compared our individual human lives to waves in the ocean. We think we're a separate entity, not realizing we're part of a much larger whole. Hanh said, "In the world of relative truth, the wave feels happy as she swells, and she feels sad when she falls. She may think, 'I am high,' or 'I am low,' and develop a superiority or inferiority complex. But when the wave touches her true nature—which is water—all her complexes will cease, and she will transcend birth and death."

Of the many spiritual teachings about the sacredness of water, one of the wisest comes from the Tao Te Ching, a 2,500-year-old text attributed to a Chinese sage named Lao Tzu. It's a manual for how to live in harmony with the Tao, which is sometimes translated as the Way or the Path. The Tao is formless, silent, and ever present, an energy that pervades the universe. It can't really be described in words, as the famous first lines of the Tao Te Ching admit:

> The Tao that can be told is not the eternal Tao.
> The name that can be named is not the eternal name.

The Tao Te Ching uses water as its central metaphor to describe this mysterious Tao. Consider these lines:

> Under heaven nothing is more soft and yielding than
>   water.
> Yet for attacking the solid and strong, nothing is better;
> It has no equal.
> The weak can overcome the strong;
> The supple can overcome the stiff.

The teaching "Be like water" is one of Taoism's foundational precepts, an idea that entered popular culture through the martial arts practitioner and film star Bruce Lee. As a brash young fighter, he was always clashing with his master, who kept telling him he was too hot-headed. After one particularly fiery exchange, his teacher sent him home with instructions that he was simply to think, and not train, for an entire week. Too restless to follow his master's advice, Lee went sailing, but there also his mind kept getting the better of him. In frustration he clenched his fist and punched the water—and that became the turning point of his life, as he suddenly realized what his master was trying to teach him. On the surface water is weak and yielding, but in reality it is one of the strongest forces on earth. From that moment, Lee resolved to empty his mind of anger, be adaptable, and flow where there is opportunity—like water.

Taoism gives us hints of how to live in harmony with the Tao through the concept of *wu wei*, which means something like "effortless action" or "the action of nonaction." *Wu wei* has similarities to *flow*, the term used to describe the state of mind that occurs when we lose all sense of time and are fully caught up in whatever we're doing. In that state, we don't need to think because effort comes naturally. To illustrate the concept of *wu wei*, philosopher Alan Watts used the example of someone trying to cross a body of water. You can use a rowboat, which is slow and hard, or you can put up a sail and catch the wind so that you glide across the water with little effort. That is the essence of *wu wei*—aligning our efforts with the Tao so that life flows smoothly.

Taoism recommends seeking a way of life that is humble and grounded in integrity and goodness. Its practitioners seek balance rather than success, and self-awareness rather than external recognition. And though they place a great deal of emphasis on meditation and solitude, they're capable of decisive action when the time is right. All of this goes against what most of us have been taught in the West, which is that the key to success is to work harder and longer. If you encounter an obstacle, put your head down and plow through it. A committed Taoist, in contrast, begins a task by sitting and observing, maybe for a long time, and when he finally stands up to do the work, the task is nearly effortless because he has put himself in harmony with it.

I could never be a true Taoist because I'm way too impatient, but my time around lakes, oceans, and hot springs has given me greater insight into what it might mean to *be like water*. Through my experiences, I've begun to feel like I'm aligning myself with something larger and deeper, and that my tight grip on anxiety, anger, and fear is loosened, one wave and one paddle stroke at a time.

Water, it turns out, can be a wise teacher, and that's true whether you're a mountain person, a woods person, or not an outdoor person at all. As Lao Tzu asks:

> Who can wait quietly while the mud settles?
> Who can remain still until the moment of action?

WOODLAND IDYLL

In keeping with the unwritten ethic of hot springs, I'm not going to tell you where our best experience with sacred water occurred, other than it's somewhere in the Cascade Range. Like many springs in Oregon, the place isn't well marked, and the directions in the old, out-of-print guidebook I was using weren't very clear. We turned off a highway and onto a secondary road, then an even narrower one. After taking a wrong turn, we retraced our steps as I referred to the directions once again.

"It's just a mile ahead," I told Bob. "Or at least I think so."

We pulled into a small parking lot cut out of the forest, and Bob parked the car next to a pickup truck whose driver was just getting out of the cab. "Is this the way to the hot spring?" I asked the young woman, who was wearing only a bathing suit.

She nodded, a wide smile lighting up her face. "It is!" she exclaimed. "You've never been here before?"

"No, we haven't," I said.

She smiled even more broadly, seemingly delighted by our answer. "Well, welcome!" she said, motioning for us to follow her onto a path that led into the woods. Whoever she was, she was certainly enthusiastic about life.

We walked into the forest, eventually coming to a river, a fairly modest-sized one by Oregon standards, and then continued on the trail that hugged its bank. The moss-draped trees around us grew steadily larger and more gnarled. After about a quarter mile we came to a place in the river where a side pool had been created out of stones. If we'd been by ourselves we likely would have turned back before we reached it because it was farther than the directions in the old guidebook indicated.

"This is it!" our impromptu guide exclaimed, as proud as if she'd created the pool by herself.

We stripped down to our swimsuits and slipped into the water, which was just the right temperature for soaking. I leaned my head back against the pool's rock border, gazing upward into the bright sunlight filtering through the trees. Just beyond our pool was the main current of the river, which rushed and burbled in a constant soothing hum. I gave a sigh of pleasure. After our earlier disappointments with hot springs, the last two pools had made me fall in love with them again.

The young woman was having her own joyous union with the water, slipping underneath the surface and then reemerging with a beatific smile on her face. "Oh, yes," she said. "I remember this."

While we'd exchanged pleasantries on our walk to this spot, the well-being seeping into our consciousness from the scenery and warm water shifted our conversation to a deeper level. Soon we started swapping life stories, including how we'd ended up in this remote spot. The young woman said she'd discovered the spring when she used to live in the area. Now she lives three hours away, but she'd driven back that day just to visit the spring. She told us about her fiancé and said they hoped to be married at this very spot with just an officiant and a photographer. She asked how long Bob and I had been married, and when I said thirty-four years her eyes widened, making me feel like Methuselah. "I hope I'll be married as long as you guys!" she exclaimed.

I steered the conversation to my writing project and asked if she thought this spring was a holy place.

Her elfin features lit up. "Oh, yes!" she exclaimed. "That's exactly right! How can this place *not* be holy?" Her arms opened wide, encompassing the beauty that surrounded us.

She'd been raised in a fundamentalist family, she went on, and had been baptized in the Jordan River in Israel as a young adult on a church trip. Her description matched my own memories of the site, and when I told her that we might have even been there at the same time, she nodded in agreement. In her worldview, it was almost certain that we'd been there at the same time.

Her spiritual path, however, had led her away from the church she was raised in, in part due to the fallout from an abusive first marriage. "I still love Jesus, but now my church is this," she said, gesturing around her once again. "He tells us to knock and the door will open for us. I truly believe that. It opens in places like this, especially."

When she heard Bob was a philosopher, she described her own personal philosophy, which primarily consisted of believing that if she thought about something hard enough, she could manifest it. She talked about how she'd been able to manifest a wonderful new life after her divorce, for example, including meeting her fiancé.

By now my skin was getting wrinkled and the sun was inching toward late afternoon. Bob had left the pool a while before, his patience with soaking exhausted, though he'd listened to our conversation from a nearby log. I sensed he'd found the conversation as intriguing as I had. The young woman had begun to seem more and more like a part of the hot spring itself, as if she was a water spirit we'd happened to intersect with by divine providence.

I reluctantly pulled myself out of the water and looked down at our guide, who was smiling as she floated in the water.

"Enjoy the rest of your visit," I said. "It's been a pleasure spending time with you. And good luck with your wedding."

"We're going to be very happy," she said, clearly getting a head start on manifesting a good marriage.

Bob and I set off down the forest path back to our car, smiling at our hot springs experience. "Wasn't that wonderful?" I asked Bob. "Such a lovely person she is."

"Oh, yes," he agreed. "I did think her philosophy was a little thin, though, especially all that stuff about being able to manifest whatever she wanted."

"Well, you do realize she's a water nymph, don't you?" I asked, stopping to look at him. "Think about it. She showed up just when we needed a guide. She led us right to the spring. And she kept us entranced for an hour with her stories. You can't expect her to have a systematic philosophy—she's a nature sprite, for goodness' sake."

We continued on our way, good-naturedly arguing about what kind of philosophy a water nymph would have. As we walked through the shafts of light created by the tall trees, I realized that whatever had happened at the hot spring, the young woman had indeed manifested a blessing for us.

Across the globe, the entrances to caves have long been considered liminal spaces between worlds. (Photo credit: Bob Sessions)

7

Caves: Dunbar Cave in Tennessee

In 1948, country music star Roy Acuff made an unusual business purchase: Dunbar Cave northwest of Nashville. He wasn't much interested in the cave itself but instead in the area just in front of its entrance, which during the summer was cooled by air blowing out of the cavern. Being a smart promoter as well as a performer, Acuff realized that the site's natural acoustics and cave-fueled air-conditioning would make it an attractive place for outdoor concerts and dances. He constructed a golf course nearby, and soon Dunbar Cave was drawing thousands of visitors for Grand Ole Opry entertainers ranging from Minnie Pearl and Ernest Tubb to the Smoky Mountain Boys. On hot summer nights the sounds of "Wabash Cannonball" and "Tennessee Waltz" drifted back into the cave, no doubt startling the bats that lived within its depths.

Even before its rebirth as a music destination, however, the cave had long drawn visitors. They explored its winding passageways first with torches, then lanterns, and later with flashlights, marveling at the stalactites hanging from its ceiling and pools of water that reflected the light in strange ways. Many scratched their names on the walls, leaving a record of human encroachment stretching back hundreds of years. Between the entertainment events and the cave explorations, Dunbar Cave was a happening place.

But all the while the cave's greatest treasures went unnoticed—until one day in 2005 when the story of Dunbar Cave took an unexpected twist.

I'm among the countless humans who are both fascinated and frightened of caves. Even in an age with sophisticated lighting and safety equipment, they're among the most disorienting of all natural environments. Cut off from the sun, often highly complex in structure, and holding a myriad of ways to get lost, hurt, or killed, caves take us away from our normal landmarks and thrust us into a different world. They're liminal spaces (from the Latin word *limen*, meaning "threshold"), marking the border between the worlds of sunlight and darkness, the known and unknown.

All the characteristics that make caves so difficult to explore also appeal to the spiritual imagination, which is why they are among humanity's oldest holy sites. With their peculiar acoustics and unusual mineral and rock formations, through the millennia they've often been viewed as the realm of the dead, spirits, or gods, their shadowy passageways full of unseen forces. Many cultures, including the Pueblo, Hopi, and Lakota, trace their origins to caves, believing that their people emerged into the light after being gestated in subterranean darkness.

While rock shelters or shallow caves were often occupied by early humans, that's not the case with true caves, which are defined as having three forms of light: sunlight at their entrance, twilight in their vestibules, and full darkness in their interiors. Instead, these dark-zone areas were typically visited mainly for ceremonial reasons, including burial of the dead and drawing and painting in chambers deep beneath the surface. "The fact that for more than 20,000 years some people went underground for their ceremonies is . . . evidence of the longest-lasting religion in the history of the world," writes Jean Clottes, an archaeologist specializing in prehistoric art.

In other words, if you want to know where religion began, head underground.

The discovery that placed Dunbar Cave within this long spiritual tradition happened when a small group of cave explorers and park officials were touring its interior in 2005 and noticed some markings that seemed out of place among the many that had been made during the historic era (carvings like "Jim + Christine 4/8/72" weren't hard to date). Among the most intriguing was a charcoal drawing of two circles, each with crosses inside, and another of a reclining human-like figure. The group took pictures of them and sent them to Jan Simek, a professor of anthropology at the University of Tennessee who specializes in prehistoric cave art. Intrigued, Simek made his own visit to the cave. His verdict? The designs weren't made by partying teenagers. Instead, they were likely created between seven hundred and a thousand years ago, making them among the most significant examples of prehistoric cave art in the United States.

Further investigations revealed more than thirty other prehistoric drawings and etchings in the passageways of Dunbar Cave. They include circles, stars, and swastikas (an ancient symbol later co-opted by the Nazis), as well as the humanoid image, which is thought to be a supernatural warrior. The people who created these markings were part of a culture archaeologists have named the Mississippian, which lasted from approximately 900 to 1600 CE. Its center was Cahokia, a city along the Mississippi River near what is now St. Louis. At its height it had more than thirty thousand inhabitants, making it comparable in size to the London and Paris of its day. At Cahokia and settlements that included Ocmulgee in Georgia, Moundville in Alabama, and Spiro Mounds in Oklahoma, people built large mounds topped by wooden structures that served as temples, residences for the elite, and burial houses for the dead. As at the Hopewell sites in Ohio, these constructions rival those of the great prehistoric monuments of Central and South America, though because they were built of earth and wood rather than stone, much of their grandeur has faded.

From these settlements the Mississippian influence spread to many sites throughout the eastern United States, where its distinctive characteristics were incorporated into types of social organization, religious beliefs, and works of art.

The discovery of the Mississippian cave art at Dunbar Cave was part of a larger scientific detective story. Prehistoric art created in the dark zone of caves—the equivalent of the famous Paleolithic paintings in French caves—was long thought to be exceedingly rare in North America. Petroglyphs (images chiseled or chipped into rocks) and pictographs (images painted onto stone surfaces with mineral pigments) are common, especially in the Southwest, but these markings are found in rock shelters or on canyon walls, not in the deep interior of true caves.

In 1979, a discovery in what came to be known as Mud Glyph Cave in eastern Tennessee rewrote the textbooks on prehistoric art in America. Cave explorers hoisted themselves into one of the cave's upper chambers, where they found walls covered with soft clay incised with many drawings. The cave's unchanging humidity had preserved the glyphs, which include a snake with horns, figures appearing to be half bird and half man, and a dancing warrior, all images that were part of Mississippian iconography. After carbon-dating the residue from cane torches found inside the chamber, researchers concluded that the glyphs were created about eight hundred years ago.

Since then, more than seventy other caves with dark-zone art have been found from Wisconsin to Florida and Virginia to Missouri. The majority are in the cavern-laced topography of the Appalachian uplands, with the greatest concentration found in middle Tennessee. Most of the sites have drawings that date to the Mississippian period between 900 and 1600 CE, but some caves have art that goes back six thousand years. The location of these sites is kept secret to protect them, which is another reason why Dunbar Cave is so exceptional; it's the only place where the general public can see this remarkable prehistoric art tradition.

As soon as I learned about its existence, I started making plans to visit Dunbar Cave.

THE UPSIDE-DOWN WORLD

When Bob and I arrived at Dunbar Cave State Park on a warm spring morning, we first saw evidence of its more recent human use—the area that hosted music events. Just outside the cave's entrance is a concrete slab where dancers once twirled, along with a raised platform for performers and a shelter where refreshments were served. Feeling the pleasantly cool breeze wafting from the cave, I could see why this would be an attractive setting for concerts, especially during humid Tennessee summers.

"Even before Roy Acuff bought Dunbar Cave, this was a popular place for events," said Adam Neblett, the park ranger who'd agreed to give us a private tour since the regular season hadn't yet started. (There are perks to being a travel writer.) "Some older people in the area still remember coming here for dances. After Acuff sold the cave, other people tried to make money off of tours, but it was never very profitable. Finally in 1973 the state of Tennessee bought it and made it into a park."

Taking a key from his pocket, Adam unlocked a padlock on the formidable gate that spans the cave's eight-by-sixteen-foot opening and led us inside. Within a few steps the bright sunlight had dimmed, and Adam told us to turn on our flashlights as we ventured deeper into the darkness, explaining that electric lighting isn't used here because it would damage the cave's ecosystem. Scanning the passageway in front of us with my flashlight, I could see that the cave's interior was dry, though in the distance I could hear the sound of water. I picked my steps carefully, having a sense that this wasn't an environment to approach casually.

"The cave entrance was occupied on and off for many thousands of years," Adam continued. "Artifacts found there include a Paleo Period projectile point from ten thousand years ago. In the cave itself, we know that prehistoric people explored its eight miles of passageways because of the residue left behind from the torches they used. But it was the discovery of the Mississippian cave art in 2005 that revolutionized our understanding of Dunbar Cave."

The first priority of officials was to protect the drawings, he said, which in other caves have been vandalized or even stolen by thieves chipping them off the walls. For more than a year they didn't say anything to the public while they waited to have a sturdy gate installed at the entrance. Once they could control access, they announced the discovery at a press conference and changed their tours to reflect this important archaeological discovery.

As we ventured farther into the cave, Adam tried to help us understand the worldview of those who had created the drawings. "The Mississippian people lived in a three-part cosmos," he explained. "Supernatural beings occupied the upper and lower worlds, while humans lived in the middle world. Caves were the entrance into that lower realm. You had to be brave to enter them because they were dangerous both physically and spiritually."

About a hundred yards later we came to the source of the water sounds I'd heard: an underground river about three feet across, its origin and exit shrouded in darkness. "Water was thought to mark the entrance into the spirit world," said Adam as we stood on a platform overlooking the inky water. "This underground river would have reinforced the impression that they were entering another realm." I thought of the River Styx in Greek mythology, the underground stream that separated the world of the living from that of the dead. It didn't take much imagination to picture the supernatural ferryman Charon rowing his boat out of the darkness toward us.

We continued our tour, the route before us winding and twisting, with ceilings occasionally low enough that we needed to crouch low. As we journeyed deeper, I had an experiential sense for what Adam was talking about. Even with my modern worldview, I had a sense we were in a different realm. I clutched my flashlight, conscious of how vulnerable I would be if I was the only one in the cave and its batteries died.

About fifteen minutes later we came to the markings that had revolutionized the understanding of Dunbar Cave. As Adam pointed them out with his flashlight, I could see why the drawings had escaped notice for so many years, hidden as they were amid the scratches, marks, and names left by more-recent cave visitors. (Here, as in many places, the sacred hides in plain sight.) The first set of markings was a circle about eight inches in diameter that looked like a sun with radiating points; it was next to another circle that was similar in size and outline but with a tail-like appendage. Both had crosses inside of them, though in the latter circle it was swirled, almost as if it were spinning.

"These two emblems have been found in many places where the Mississippian people lived," Adam said. "They might refer to the structure of the universe, with the first image representing the relationship between the earth and the sun deity and the second one a comet or shooting star representing the underworld, which is kind of an upside-down version of what lies above. But like any interpretation of prehistoric art, these are just educated guesses."

Walking a few more yards, he showed us a seven-foot-long anthropomorphic image that is thought to depict a supernatural being of some sort, a figure with both human and animal characteristics and a weapon extending from its head. "The Cherokee are one of the cultural descendants of the Mississippian people," he said. "It's quite possible that this figure is related to their traditional stories of guiding and protective spirits."

We headed deeper into the cave, and as we picked our steps with care I thought about how brave you'd have to be to enter this environment with only a reed torch, knowing that gods and spirits were waiting for you.

ART IN THE DARK

My time in Dunbar Cave brought to mind my first encounter
with prehistoric art, when I toured a reproduction of the famed
Lascaux Cave in southwestern France. Because the original is
too precious to have tourists traipsing through it, officials have
constructed a replica experience that gives visitors a sense of its
interior. The tour was in French, so I missed the commentary,
but the visuals were so stunning that I was actually grateful
not to be distracted by the guide's words. The cave walls were
adorned with designs that seemed almost magical—galloping
horses, massive bulls, fierce bison, all on rough stone surfaces,
sometimes high on the cave walls beyond ordinary reach. The
paintings and etchings showed a remarkable artistic sophistica-
tion for so-called primitive people, with shading, perspective,
and the illusion of movement. It was easy to imagine how powerful they must have seemed to the people who visited them by
the flickering light of torches.

The Paleolithic cave art of Europe represents the earliest
and the longest-lasting religious tradition in the world. We
can only speculate why people created these markings. Perhaps
they believed that the animal spirits were already there, inside
the walls, and that drawing or touching them was a way of preparing for an upcoming hunt. Maybe they illustrate the visions
of shamans, or mark places where initiation rituals were held.
The reasons for their creation will always elude us, but few can
deny they are among the most remarkable works of art ever
created. Even after two decades, I can still see the Lascaux art
when I close my eyes—and when I stood in Dunbar Cave in
Tennessee, I felt an echo of their power.

That said, I must admit that the Mississippian art of the
eastern United States doesn't have the beauty of the Paleolithic
art of France. But it does have its own symbolic sophistica-
tion, according to Jan Simek, the cave specialist from the University of Tennessee who first authenticated the Dunbar Cave
art. After exploring dozens of caves, Simek and his team have
discovered a general pattern of designs. Those closer to cave

entrances tend to be more realistic—figures of humans holding bows, for example—while those in the deepest interiors contain more enigmatic markings.

Beau Carroll, an archaeologist who is a member of the Eastern Band of Cherokee Indians, has written about Cherokee beliefs relating to caves and tribal connections to some of the markings that have been found. According to him, Cherokee tradition says there is another world like ours that exists below the earth but that its seasons are backward, which is why during the summer months caves are cooler than outside air, and in the winter, warmer. "Caves are often mentioned in Cherokee myths, and this is where many supernatural beings live," he writes. "To go into a cave would mean a chance of disrespecting whatever deity lived there and would be very dangerous. Only the most skilled medicine men or warriors would risk an encounter with one of these creatures."

His words gave me even more respect for those who ventured into this upside-down world.

All of this raises a question: Why should we care that these markings exist? Few people today, after all, believe that supernatural forces occupy caves or that we can get in touch with animal spirits by painting them on walls. Besides that, caves are sort of creepy, aren't they? They're dank and scary. Bats live in them. Even on a guided tour, caves emanate a sense of danger, which those who suffer from claustrophobia sense better than anyone, as irrational as those fears can appear.

But my experiences in Dunbar Cave make me believe that contemporary humans shouldn't dismiss caves so readily as places of spiritual power. My reasons have something to do with the importance of *embodied* spirituality. Being in the cave made me realize how almost all of my most significant spiritual experiences have had a physical trigger: Stepping inside a cathedral, for example, and being overwhelmed by the echoing interior space. Standing on the edge of a canyon, watching the light play across its peaks and valleys. Walking on a beach and hearing the waves crash rhythmically, wordlessly speaking of something vast and deep. I felt something similar when we entered the twilight zone of Dunbar Cave and then headed into darkness lit only by our small flashlights. There was spiritual power there that I could feel in my bones.

What helps explain what I experienced in Dunbar Cave, I think, is the universal human need for myths. The modern world too often equates *myth* with *lie*, but a better formulation, to use an old truism, is that some truths are so large that only a myth can contain them. That's why the great myths of antiquity still speak to us, from the Greek story of the death of Icarus who flew too close to the sun to the Norse tales of the end of the world known as Ragnarok. Entering the cave propelled me into an experience of myth, including when I stood by the underground stream and thought of Charon rowing his boat on the River Styx. As a human, I'm primed by millennia of evolution to try to make sense of frightening places, which is exactly what myths attempt to do.

Myths across many cultures explore the journey from light into darkness, which can be either literal or figurative. While we don't often find ourselves lost in a cave, being lost in interior darkness is all too common. Myths give us inspiration for how to deal with this terror, which is often personified as a fearsome creature such as a dragon. (The half man–half bull figure of the Minotaur who lived in a cave on the island of Crete is another example.) These monsters guard treasures that can only be captured by those of great courage and determination. It's no wonder that the pioneering psychologist Carl Jung, who developed the theory of archetypes that are formed in the collective unconscious, viewed caves as symbols of great spiritual significance.

During my own mythic journey into Dunbar Cave—during which I encountered not even a baby dragon, unfortunately—I thought of my experiences with Zoom church, realizing afresh why they left me so disheartened. I've always believed that a spiritual journey should be an adventure full of risks and challenges (which is a lesson, of course, reinforced by countless myths). But while Christianity has powerful stories that can

hold their own among the greatest narratives of religious history, much of contemporary liturgy seems pale and wan, especially when experienced in the antiseptic confines of the digital
world. Perhaps that's why even thoroughly modern humans
like myself can feel a déjà-vu shiver in our souls when we enter
a cave, that ancient place for encountering spirits.

"Where you stumble, there lies your treasure," wrote scholar
of mythology Joseph Campbell. "The very cave you are afraid
to enter turns out to be the source of what you are looking for."

HAVENS FOR THE HOLY

Caves continued to be spiritual sanctuaries long after the prehistoric era ended. Elijah heard the voice of God at the entrance
to a cave, and Muhammad received his first divine revelations
in another. According to Eastern Orthodox tradition, Jesus was
born in a cave, which was a common place to shelter animals
in his day, and all branches of the Christian faith believe that
Jesus was resurrected in a tomb, which is a kind of cave. Holy
people in many traditions, especially Buddhism and Hinduism, have often lived in caves, drawing pilgrims who seek their
wisdom. In Christianity, many churches were built on top of
caves sacred to earlier traditions, and to this day many cathedrals have underground crypts.

Grottos—which are either constructed or naturally
formed—are a specialized type of cave associated with worship. The word came into English via the Italian *grotta*, which
in turn was derived from the Latin *crypta* and Greek *krypte*,
meaning a "hidden place." (The old TV show *Tales from the
Crypt* comes immediately to mind.) In the pagan Greek and
Roman worlds, grottos often held shrines to local deities. The
practice continued in Christianity, especially Roman Catholi-
cism. Throughout Europe I've seen grottos in many out-of-
the-way places, typically a niche in a rock that holds a statue of
the Virgin Mary or Jesus, often with offerings of fresh flowers
that show the shrine is still in active use.

Fascination with grottos got a major boost in 1858 when a French girl named Bernadette Soubirous saw the Virgin Mary standing in a niche in a rock outcropping outside the town of Lourdes, the first of a series of visions. Devotion to Our Lady of Lourdes spread throughout the Catholic world, leading many parishes and individuals to create their own grottos dedicated to her. When you see an overturned bathtub in someone's front yard sheltering a Mary statue with hands outstretched, you're seeing an echo of Lourdes and, beyond that, perhaps a flicker of what those prehistoric humans experienced when they entered the caves of Lascaux. Inside the darkness of a cave, sacred mystery awaits.

The contemporary world has largely lost its fascination with caves, forgetting that for most of human history they were places of magnetic attraction. Many people avoid caves altogether, and those who do visit mostly gravitate to commercial caves with dramatic formations of stalactites, crystals, and minerals. The idea that caves could have a spiritual aspect is largely forgotten—unless you happen to have a tour of Dunbar Cave and at a bend in a passageway you get a shiver up your back that comes unbidden, hinting of powerful forces within the darkness.

Of all the myths relating to caves, the most famous comes to us from the Greek philosopher Plato, who in *The Republic* recounts the Allegory of the Cave as taught by Socrates. The world, Socrates said, is like a deep cave where a group of prisoners is kept in chains. Lit only by the dim light of a fire, the cave has flickering shadows on its walls that the prisoners mistake for the real world. One day a prisoner escapes and is amazed by what he sees in the world above. When he returns to the cave to tell his fellow prisoners what he has seen, however, they refuse to believe him. So it is with humans, Socrates concludes. We live in a cave, and only a few enlightened souls can see that the dramas we experience are just dancing shadows on the walls. The myth has been influential for millennia, teaching us that enlightenment comes when we realize that our understanding of reality is based upon illusion.

But there's another cave tradition that I find equally compelling, this one associated with the Kogi, an Indigenous people who live high in the Sierra Nevada de Santa Marta Mountains of Colombia. Their traditional way of forming their spiritual leaders is that soon after birth, a few children of each generation are taken away to live inside a dimly lit cave. Their mothers continue to care for them, but in other ways they lead lives of low light and sensory deprivation. Theirs is a childhood without sunlight, rain, or growing plants. They eat bland, tasteless foods, and the only sounds they hear are soft and subdued. As the children age, the elders of the tribe begin to teach them, coming into the cave with stories of the beautiful mountains that lie outside, of snow and wind and birds that circle high above, but the children's knowledge of this world is only secondhand.

Now you're probably thinking that this is a cruel child-rearing practice and that someone who did this in our society would rightly have their children taken away from them. But that's not the end of the story. When the children are nine years old, they are led out of the cave into the sunlight. Boys and girls who have known only the dimly lit cave see for the first time the incredible, stunning mountain vistas ahead of them. They hear birdsongs, smell flowers heavy with perfume, eat foods rich with flavor, and feel warm rain on their faces for the first time.

During their time in the cave and in the years that follow, these children learn spiritual techniques for maintaining harmony in both the natural and human world. But their most important lesson comes from their experience of living in the cave and then emerging into the light: they know that this world is beautiful beyond their imaginings.

Now I don't think we should raise children in caves, and I don't agree with Socrates that what we experience is just flickers on a cave wall. But after my time in Dunbar Cave I found myself thinking of both these stories, pondering what I'd experienced in Tennessee. I could see the parallels between my time in the cave and going through the pandemic: both entailed going into darkness and being at the mercy of unknown and dangerous forces. During the past year it had often seemed as if I was chained in a cave, watching the flickering lights on the wall as I tried to discern what was reality and what was illusion. So much of what I'd learned about the pandemic was confusing and contradictory, with the added anxiety of political unrest and controversy. There were many months when my chains were heavy indeed.

But now that the pandemic was easing its grip, it was the Kogi story that was starting to speak to me more. What had I learned, there in the darkness of the cave? I thought of those nine-year-olds (a number that parallels the nine months a baby spends in the womb) emerging into the light for the first time. For the rest of their lives they would never take the middle world for granted, to use the Mississippian term. I thought of all the things I vowed never to take for granted again, from browsing the shelves of our library and eating in a restaurant to attending funerals and weddings. As the virus began to ebb, I had a sense of stepping into the sunshine outside of a cave. I didn't want to lose my appreciation for the everyday miracles of ordinary life, I realized. I didn't want to go back to my world just as it had been before; I wanted to take the lessons of the cave with me, just as the Kogi children do.

Inside a cave, we place ourselves at risk, both physically and spiritually, even if we don't believe in animal spirits inhabiting the walls. But the potential reward for a journey into darkness is transformation—which is something to remember when we're lost in an inner labyrinth, trying to find our way back to the sunlight.

We explored the depths of Dunbar Cave for a couple of hours, marveling at its complex topography of twisting passageways, chambers hung with stalactites, and pools of water that reflected the light of our flashlights in eerie ways. As we began our journey back to the surface, I asked Adam what had happened to the Mississippian people who created the art in the cave.

"Mississippian culture was in decline even before European contact, for reasons we don't know, and its center at Cahokia was mostly abandoned by 1250," he said. "But the Mississippian people are believed to be the ancestors of many of today's tribes who live in the eastern United States, including the Cherokee, Creeks, and Natchez."

As we passed by the first drawings Adam had shown us, he stopped and directed our attention to the opposite wall, pointing out a couple of small, faint marks. "These symbols are Cherokee syllabary, which is the written form of their language," he said. "This system was created in the 1820s, about ten years before they were forced to leave this part of the country on the Trail of Tears in 1838. While this set of syllabary isn't dated, others in the cave are marked with the date 1855, which indicates that a generation after the forced removal, some of them came back."

There's a story, he continued, that during the exodus to Oklahoma a group of Cherokee made a detour to visit a sacred cave a few miles off of their route. It's not known where that cave was, but it may have been Dunbar Cave. "Perhaps they were saying goodbye, or maybe they did a ceremony here," Adam said. "We don't know exactly what these symbols in the cave mean. Translating early syllabary is difficult even for native speakers. There are multiple dialects of the language, and not knowing which dialect the writer spoke complicates this. These symbols could be names of people or perhaps something else. In another cave in Alabama, inscriptions in syllabary are thought to represent sounds rather than words, and they can't be shared with outsiders because they are sacred. Some knowledge can be shared, but some is reserved for Cherokee people only."

Sounds rather than words. Adam's words reverberated in my mind as we continued walking. I knew from long experience that what is most important often can't be communicated through words. I thought of the Hindu belief that the world came into being with the sacred sound OM, which is used to this day in ceremonies and meditation, an echo of the sound that began the cosmos.

At last a speck of sunlight became visible, a pinpoint that grew in brightness and size as we approached the mouth of the cave. I was grateful that I'd been able to glimpse a few of the mysteries of the subterranean world of Dunbar Cave. I knew I could never fully understand them, not only because they were of a culture not my own but also because I think no one can fully understand them. Caves, more than any other place I'd visited during my quest to find the sacred in America, don't yield their secrets easily.

Even after returning to the middle world, I knew I would long ponder my time in the realm of the spirits.

The majestic buffalo, the largest mammal in North America, once roamed in vast herds across the Great Plains of the United States. (PHOTO CREDIT: TRAVEL SOUTH DAKOTA)

8

Animals: The Buffalo Roundup in South Dakota

My experiences in Dunbar Cave settled deep into my psyche, stirring up more memories of seeing the prehistoric cave art in France. One part of Lascaux Cave in particular kept coming back to me, an area known as the Hall of Bulls. Located in a chamber that could hold about fifty people, its largest paintings are of aurochs, an extinct species of the wild cattle family. The images range from thirteen to sixteen feet in length, animals that are so realistic you can practically hear them snort and paw the earth. They gallop and prance across the uneven surfaces of the cave in works created by people who knew not only how these animals looked but also how they moved. Though the last auroch died in Poland in 1627, their spirit lives on in this sacred cave.

Even in painted form, the Lascaux bulls have a power much greater than that of the mild-mannered dairy cows my father milked each morning and evening of my childhood. Domesticated cattle have had almost all of the wildness bred out of them, but for much of human history bulls were fierce creatures of great spiritual significance. In ancient Mesopotamian mythology, for example, the hero Gilgamesh has an epic battle with the Bull of Heaven, while the Greeks had the story of the Minotaur, that blend of bull and man who lived in a labyrinth on the island of Crete. In the Bible, people started worshiping a golden calf while Moses was up on the mountain talking to God, a reflection of the bull worship that was common in many neighboring cultures.

Animals clearly fascinated our ancestors. It's telling, for example, that about 99 percent of European Paleolithic cave paintings are of animals, often very realistic and detailed, while the few humans that are featured are merely variations of stick figures. In the ensuing millennia animals continued to play an important role in people's spiritual lives. (It's no accident that our word *animal* comes from the Latin *anima*, which means "soul.") Shamanism, which is a set of practices common to many Indigenous cultures across the world, believes that animal spirits can assist humans. Shamans go into trances to connect with these spirits, bringing back information that helps them in this realm. Some of the earliest ritual sites excavated by archaeologists feature animal skulls, often of bears, while animals populate mythologies ranging from the owls associated with the Greek goddess Athena to the four sacred animals of ancient China (the azure dragon, the vermilion bird, the white tiger, and the black tortoise).

Many mythologies include creatures that blend animal and human characteristics such as the warrior figure I'd seen in Dunbar Cave. The technical term for this is *therianthrope*, from the Greek words for *beast* and *human*. Ancient Egypt had many such gods, including Thoth, the ibis-headed god of wisdom, and Sekhmet, whose ferocity was reflected in her lion's head. While centaurs and mermaids, both therianthropes, have fallen out of fashion, popular culture has an enduring fascination with werewolves and vampires.

Looking back on my travels, I realized I'd encountered sacred animals a surprising number of times, from the Marching Bears of Effigy Mounds to the Great Serpent Mound in Ohio. The sandhill crane migration introduced me to Asian traditions regarding sacred birds, while Pipestone National

Monument taught me the story of White Buffalo Calf Woman, who gave the ceremonial pipe to the Lakota. I found it intriguing that she took the form of an animal that is an evolutionary cousin of the aurochs from the Hall of Bulls in Lascaux.

THE BULLS OF THE GREAT PLAINS

I have my own connection to sacred animals through buffalo, who in a sense are part of my family tree. That's because my late father-in-law, Bill Sessions, was employed by the state of South Dakota as a veterinarian for more than a decade, during which he helped oversee the health of Custer State Park's buffalo herd, one of the largest in the nation. Bill wasn't a sentimental man, but he had a deep, hard-earned admiration for these animals, an affection that he passed along to me.

The term *buffalo* is actually a misnomer for the creatures that once roamed by the millions across the Great Plains. Buffalo are native to South Asia and Africa, while bison are native to North America and Europe. Though they're related, bison have beards and a hump at their shoulders, while buffalo do not. But because the term buffalo is so common in North America, the two terms tend to be used interchangeably.

Bill loved to tell stories about bison, who are exceptionally strong, agile, and fast. Despite their bulk (the males can exceed two thousand pounds), they're able to run up to thirty-five miles per hour and can survive weather ranging from blazing summer heat to fierce blizzards. One of Bill's favorite tales was about a clueless tourist who was driving through Custer State Park one day in a Volkswagen Beetle. He came up behind a large bull bison standing in the middle of the road and honked his horn to get him to move. The bison didn't budge, so the man honked again. This time the animal turned his huge head around, came over to the car, and methodically destroyed it with his sharp horns and hooves. Bill said the bull took his time and was quite thorough. The driver, fortunately, escaped unharmed, but he learned a valuable lesson about bison.

Bill was especially fond of working the annual Buffalo Roundup, when the animals are brought into corrals for a veterinarian checkup and sorting. Because the park's grasslands can support only about a thousand bison and new calves are born each spring, each year several hundred are sold at auction. In the weeks before the roundup, herdsmen start gathering them in from the rangeland. (If you're wondering how you herd bison, the answer is very carefully.) Then on the morning of the roundup, in front of more than twenty thousand spectators who've gotten up at zero-dark-thirty to get there, the cowboys bring them the last mile into the corrals, whooping and hollering as the animals gallop at full speed.

The Buffalo Roundup is organized by humans, but it's an echo of what once happened naturally. When Europeans first came to North America, it's estimated that more than thirty million bison roamed the interior of the continent in herds up to twenty miles in width and sixty miles in length. For millennia, the species provided sustenance for the native peoples of North America. From nose to tail, every part of the animal could be used. In addition to providing food, the bones were made into tools, hooves boiled for glue, bladders were made into water containers, and hides were fashioned into moccasins, clothing, and tipis. Even the dried dung was useful, as it provided a valuable source of fuel on the treeless prairie.

By the late 1800s, the once-plentiful bison teetered on the edge of extinction, a consequence of what historian Dan Flores calls a "perfect storm" of factors that included a changing climate, growing competition for grass and water from horses, loss of habitat, new bovine diseases, and an ever-larger population of human hunters. In the latter decades of the nineteenth century, the booming market for buffalo robes sealed their fate. The U.S. government did little to mitigate the slaughter, recognizing that without the sustenance provided by the buffalo herds, subduing the Indigenous tribes of the Great Plains would be easier. Some of the most heart-wrenching photos of the era show stacks of thousands of buffalo skulls piled high. Much of the time, the hides were taken east to be sold and the rest of the animal was left to rot, a tragic contrast to the Native American ethic of using everything from the animal. By 1900, there were less than a thousand bison left.

Thankfully, grassroots efforts to save the species were launched by a variety of people, from Mary Ann Goodnight, who persuaded her rancher husband to rescue a few orphaned buffalo calves for her to raise, to Theodore Roosevelt, who cofounded the American Bison Society. We owe thanks as well to Yellowstone National Park and Custer State Park, which have sent breeding stock to ranches around the continent. Gradually the bison population has grown, and today the animals are raised throughout the West, including on tribal lands. The InterTribal Buffalo Council, a group of sixty-nine federally recognized tribes from nineteen states, has a mission to restore buffalo to territories governed by Indigenous people. Herds ranging in size from under ten to more than a thousand bison now graze on nearly one million acres of tribal land. This represents not only an environmental success story but a spiritual rebirth as well, because the buffalo is still considered a sacred animal by many tribes.

The complex story of the American bison was on my mind as Bob and I traveled in mid-September to attend the Buffalo Roundup in Custer State Park, the event my father-in-law had told me about decades before. Our route took us west across the fertile plains of Iowa and then into South Dakota. Once we crossed the Missouri River the land switched from farms to ranches, the same grasslands that sustained the buffalo for millennia. Because Bob's family is from the Black Hills, I've made that trip many times, but I never come out of the Missouri River valley without feeling my spirits lift as we finally enter the West.

"First one to see an antelope gets five dollars," I said, which is what I always say at this point in the journey. Rituals are important, including on car trips.

I'd wanted to experience the Buffalo Roundup ever since I first heard my father-in-law's stories about it. By the time I met him, Bill had already retired from his veterinary career, but his experiences with bison were among his favorite memories. He often recounted them after hearing news reports of tourists getting hurt by bison in Custer State Park, which happens occasionally despite the best efforts of the park staff. The desire to take a selfie with a buffalo can overcome even the most intensive public education effort.

Two hours from the Missouri River we first saw the jagged ridges of Badlands National Park in the distance, then we continued west to the Black Hills, the forested, ancient mountain range that lines the western border of the state. As we drove higher into the hills the air grew cooler and the landscape more scenic, with the autumn yellows of the aspens forming a bright contrast to the olive-green ponderosa pines. After setting up camp outside the town of Custer, we headed to bed early, knowing that morning was going to come too soon.

The next day it was still dark when we left our campsite. At the entrance to Custer State Park, we joined a long line of cars heading to the viewing areas for the roundup. Everyone needed to be in place before the bison were herded into the corrals, both for our safety and theirs. The slow, stop-and-start journey took us nearly two hours, but at last we reached the designated area. After parking our car, we bundled up against the early morning chill and set off for a roped-off section that had an expansive view of the valley through which the bison would be funneled. For bison fans, this was the equivalent of a mosh pit at a music concert.

And then we waited, as we had at the sandhill crane migration, because wild animals aren't good at keeping to a schedule. The crowd was a little restless but good-natured, with some people sporting bison-themed headgear that made them look like minotaurs. Many had brought lawn chairs and were nursing thermoses of coffee as they visited with other hardy bison fans. I gave a rueful smile when I saw an ambulance stationed at the edge of the crowd. It had an image of a bull bison on its side, a powerful reminder not to pet the furry cows, as the tongue-in-cheek stickers for sale in the park's visitor center advised.

The official starting time came and went, with no explanation why the stars of the event were delayed, but finally a report circulated through the crowd that the herd was approaching. Sure enough, up on a distant hill a black spot appeared, and then another and another. Soon bison were flowing over the ridge in a living wave, so many that it was difficult to distinguish individual animals. The prairie dogs in the grass ahead of them dived for cover, a defense mechanism they've used for millennia. As the bison grew closer to the viewing area, I spared a thought for what would happen if they bolted in the wrong direction, as the flimsy ropes wouldn't stop a two-thousand-pound animal running at full speed. Thankfully the cowboys seemed to have things well under control, hooting and cracking their bull whips in the air to keep the animals moving in the right direction.

At last the leading edge of the herd passed by us, a phalanx of galloping beasts that made the ground shake with their hooves, a great cloud of dust in the air above them. The thunder-like sound reverberated in my chest, the pounding of hooves synching with the fast beating of my heart. My eyes filled with tears, just as they had during the sandhill crane flight on our last morning in Nebraska—once again, a sure sign of the sacred.

And then in a few minutes it was over. The herd disappeared over a hill, headed to the corrals where they would be examined and vaccinated, leaving in their wake a palpable sense of awe. We'd seen not only one of the largest bison herds in the world, but also an entire species that has come back from the brink of extinction.

ANIMAL WISDOM

I suspect I'm one of the few Christians who has a bear skull on her home altar. I got it from my friend Brian, who'd had it sitting in his basement for decades after purchasing it at a powwow.

"I was cleaning the basement and found this in a box," he said as he placed the interlocking jaw and upper part of the skull into my hands. "I figured you'd appreciate having it."

Why, yes, I would indeed love to have my own bear skull. What a thoughtful gift! I found a place for it among the Virgin Mary figurines, prayer cards, and other religious trinkets I've picked up on my travels around the world. As a big believer in the usefulness of spiritual paraphernalia, I was delighted to have one of the oldest tools of all on my altar, one that gave me a sense of kinship with my earliest human ancestors.

I have a fondness for many animals, from the cat and dog who share our home and the birds that flock to our feeders, to the wild animals I encounter on my travels (though I'd be happy with fewer white-tailed deer, who seem to have a death wish on Iowa highways). That bond makes it easy for me to resonate with the idea of sacred animals, which can be found in contemporary faiths as well as prehistoric ones. Cattle are considered sacred in India, for example, where they wander through cities and towns without fear of being harmed. Hindus also honor the bull Nandi, the devoted animal companion of the god Shiva, and Hanuman, the beloved god in monkey form. Many Indigenous peoples have deep ties to animals, from the Tlingit people of southeastern Alaska who regard orcas, ravens, eagles, and wolves as kin, to the Iroquois of the northeastern part of the United States, whose creation story says that the earth was created on the back of a turtle.

While Christianity doesn't have as strong a connection to animals as many religions, it has more echoes of the concept than you might realize. Jesus is often referred to as the lamb of God, a symbol that evokes both innocence and the sacrifices that were made in the Jewish Temple. A dove is a symbol of the Holy Spirit, dating back to the bird that descended upon Jesus at his baptism. Jesus reminded his followers that even though five sparrows were sold for two pennies, not one of them is forgotten in God's sight. And while St. Francis is best known for his love of animals, other saints have charming stories relating to their ties to the natural world. In the early centuries of

Christianity in Ireland, for example, St. Cuthbert became the patron saint of otters because they would warm his feet while he was praying on the edge of the sea. St. Brigid had a special affection for cows, who produced a supernatural amount of milk in her presence. And after a blackbird laid her eggs in the outstretched hand of St. Kevin while he was praying, he remained still until the eggs hatched and the fledglings flew away. These are fanciful stories, to be sure, but they point to the enduring truth that animals can be our spiritual teachers and companions.

Islam has a tradition of honoring cats that goes back to Muhammad, who kept a cat named Muezza. One day the cat fell asleep on his robe, and when it was time for him to go to prayers he cut off his sleeve to keep from disturbing Muezza. As a cat lover I'm amused by a contrasting story from the life of the Buddha that says as he was dying, all the animals came to pay him homage except for the cat, who was taking a nap.

While I love my cat Loki (who would likely greet my death with the same indifference as his ancestors did the Buddha's), I must admit that our dog Cody is probably the most spiritually advanced being in our household. Kids love to pet him because he's so calm and gentle, and when we used to take him to my mother's nursing home it was like traveling with a celebrity. Almost all the residents wanted to pet him, including the nonverbal ones in the memory care unit. We long ago dubbed him Cody-sattva, after *bodhisattva*, which is a Buddhist term for a being who refrains from entering nirvana in order to help other sentient beings become enlightened. In true bodhisattva fashion, Cody takes no pride in his exalted status and continues on his selfless mission of spreading goodwill (and copious amounts of hair) wherever he goes.

Many animals have abilities that seem to border on the supernatural, including dogs that can sense when their owners are coming home, even if their humans are on unpredictable schedules and are far beyond the reach of hearing. It's well documented that before earthquakes and tsunamis many species behave in unexpected ways, perhaps because they're able to sense underground signals that human senses don't register. Before the 2004 tsunami that killed more than 200,000 people in countries surrounding the Indian Ocean, for example, dogs refused to go outdoors, elephants and flamingos moved to higher ground, and birds stopped singing, among other peculiar behaviors. The loss of nonhuman life was surprisingly low, said biologists.

Another example of animal wisdom, though of a decidedly quirky sort, is the February 2 custom of seeing what happens when a groundhog emerges from its burrow. If it sees its shadow, winter is supposed to linger for another six weeks, but if not, spring is on its way. As Boria Sax writes in *The Mythical Zoo: Animals in Myth, Legend, and Literature*, "Nobody really pretends to take the augury seriously, but it does have very exalted roots in history and myth, going back to rural societies, in which agriculturalists watched for subtle signs such as the migration of birds or the emergence of animals from hibernation to decide on the best times for planting and harvesting. . . . Groundhog Day, while seemingly trivial, turns out to have a history as old and complex as perhaps any celebration."

The pagan Celtic holiday of Imbolc is likely one of the sources of our contemporary Groundhog Day traditions. Falling midway between the winter solstice and the spring equinox, it celebrated the return of the light and the approaching spring. After Christianity came to Ireland, the festival became connected to St. Brigid, whose name echoed that of the Celtic fire goddess Brigid. In yet another example of how religious holidays are often a potpourri of traditions, February 2 is also the Christian feast of Candlemas, which marks the presentation of Jesus in the Temple, where he was recognized as "a light for revelation to the gentiles" by the aged prophet Simeon (Luke 2:32). Because of that story, candles became associated with the day and were brought to churches for a blessing—hence the name, from "candle mass."

In the United States, a more modern layer of meaning was added to the seemingly archaic holiday with the 1993 comedy *Groundhog Day*, which has been hailed as one of the most profound spiritual movies ever made. Bill Murray plays a self-centered TV weather reporter who's sent to Punxsutawney, Pennsylvania, to cover its annual Groundhog Day celebration. He finds himself reliving the same day over and over again until he breaks the curse by learning to serve others and embrace the beauty of each moment. The deeper meanings of the film have been celebrated by Christians, Buddhists, Hindus, and members of other faith traditions, proving that even grumpy groundhogs can bear spiritual messages.

Given humanity's long history of honoring the sacred in animals, it's not surprising that our pets can be spiritual teachers (or perhaps an actual bodhisattva, as in the case of my dog). If you have companion animals in your life, you've likely learned a number of lessons from them. Maybe they've taught you patience or inspired you with their devotion. Maybe they've reminded you to laugh and find beauty in small things, or taught you about death and the transitory nature of all life. Hopefully you've learned things that make up for the vet bills, muddy footprints, hair on the sofa, and other trials of having a pet.

In the pantheon of animals with spiritual charisma, it's the powerful species such as bear, lion, bull, and elephant that get the most attention. Wolves are part of that select group as well, as I experienced on a wolf-watching trip in Yellowstone National Park one cold January. Over the years I'd seen plenty of nature documentaries on wolves, with footage of romping puppies, affectionate family members, and fierce battles between packs, but nothing could compare to the visceral thrill of seeing wild wolves in their natural habitat.

There's no better place in the world for wolf-watching than Yellowstone National Park, which is home to about a hundred of the animals. Wolves were reintroduced to the park in 1995 through a program that brought back a predator that had been systematically eradicated in Yellowstone in the first decades of the twentieth century. At the time, wolves were seen as threats to the other animals in the park as well as the cattle beyond its borders. As the years passed, however, park naturalists began to realize that a terrible mistake had been made. By removing the top predator from the Yellowstone ecosystem, the park lacked a key link in its complex web of life—and in some hard to define but significant way, the park had also lost its wildness.

The reintroduction of wolves in 1995 was controversial, but it's gone better than most park officials had dared to hope. Within Yellowstone, the wolves have had a cascade of positive effects on the park's ecosystem. By killing primarily old and sick elk, wolves have improved the quality of the herd. Grizzly bears benefit from the extra protein they get from carcasses left by wolves. Even the park's plant life has been affected, as elk that formerly fed on the tender vegetation near rivers and streams now must be more vigilant and stay on higher ground. As a result, more trees and bushes now line waterways in the park, providing additional habitat for other species.

The guide who led our program said that nearly as significant has been the star power of the wolves. "A lot of money flows into the park and surrounding area each year because of the Yellowstone wolves," she said. "People come from all over the world to see them, and some have even moved to the area just so they can observe them regularly. The locals call them puppy-razzi."

Before taking her current job, she had worked for a nonprofit foundation dedicated to saving wolves and had spent part of the year traveling with a female wolf doing educational programs in environmental centers. When I asked what it was like to live and travel so closely with one of these magnificent animals, she told several stories about the wolf's extraordinary capabilities. Like all wolves, her sense of smell was about a thousand times keener than that of a human. The wolf seemed to sense where something was physically wrong with people she met, sniffing insistently at the spot where they had an old injury, for example, or where they had been diagnosed with cancer.

Even more intriguing was a story about what happened when the guide's brother showed up at one of her programs. "I didn't have the chance to greet him beforehand, so she couldn't have known of our connection," she recalled. "But as soon as she saw him in the crowd she went right over to him and stood at his feet, then looked back at me as if she was saying, 'This one is part of your pack.'"

Our guide also spoke of the powerful emotional response some people have to being in the presence of a wolf. One man, for example, contacted her a year after attending one of her programs and said something remarkable had happened to him because of seeing the animal. Before the program, he'd been an alcoholic, struggling daily with the torment of addiction. But after being in the presence of the wolf, that terrible hunger was gone. It had been a year and it still hadn't returned, and he credited it to her.

BISON RENDEZVOUS

The guide's stories brought to mind one of my own most intense experiences with wild animals, which happened years ago when we were camping at Theodore Roosevelt National Park in North Dakota with our young sons. One night Bob and I were awakened by an odd sound: a deep, resonant rumbling that was coming from just outside our camper. When we peeked out the window, we saw about twenty bison that were passing through the campground in the dark, walking just a few feet away from us like furry, immense ghosts. It was rutting season, and the sound we'd heard came from the males, a guttural, low-frequency rumbling that was both eerie and mesmerizing. I felt a hint of danger, knowing that our canvas-sided, pop-up camper was no match for a charging bison, but at the same time the experience was thrilling.

I crossed over to where our boys were sleeping and gently shook them awake. "You need to wake up to see something," I whispered in their ears. "Just keep quiet."

Wide-eyed, they knuckled the sleep out of their eyes and peered out of the window as I pulled back the curtain, a look of wonder spreading across their faces. We watched in silence as the herd passed by to the accompaniment of the rumbling, which sometimes sounded like a lion just beginning to roar and other times like a deep purr.

"That's the sound of the wild," I whispered to my sons. "Remember this."

At last the bison herd disappeared into the night. It took all of us a while to get back to sleep, and in the morning we half-wondered whether it had been a dream—which in a way I guess it was, a dream with similarities to those experienced by the long-ago artists in the Hall of Bulls in Lascaux Cave.

At the Buffalo Roundup in South Dakota, the show wasn't over once the animals had raced past the viewing stand. Bob and I followed the crowd down to the corrals, where we watched as cowboys skillfully guided them into the area where veterinarians and their assistants waited. In their own stoic, South Dakota fashion they were clearly having the time of their lives. I could see why my father-in-law had loved this event, with its drama, energy, element of danger, and chance to be close to these magnificent animals.

The bison who were being herded into the medical area, however, were not very happy, as I discovered when I found a spot overlooking the first pen. A half dozen animals were pacing around its perimeter, snorting their displeasure and occasionally kicking at the sides of the corral so hard they made the metal shake. Up close, I marveled at their massive bodies and dense, brownish-black coats. Despite their size they were surprisingly nimble, capable of swift turns as they jostled with their companions.

"Just give them a minute," said the man running the chute. "One of them will figure out that it needs to go into the chute. And once one goes, the others will follow."

The man was right, because bison are herd animals who like to follow a leader. Soon one cow had entered the chute, and then the rest followed. The cowboy went on to explain that this characteristic aided greatly in the annual roundup, as animals that they'd missed would eventually find their way to the corrals of their own accord. "They'll stand outside the gate waiting to be let in, because they want to be with the rest of the herd," he said.

I stood for a long time by the pen, fascinated by the behaviors of each new mix of animals. Some were relatively docile, while others—even the young calves—were hard to handle. Most impressive of all were the bulls, who stood more than six feet tall and a dozen feet long. I watched as the bison were divided into two groups, with mature animals going for a quick checkup in one area and calves sent to another for tagging, branding, vaccinating, and deworming. Even with machine-powered vises that held the animals tight as they were being worked on, I could see that the workers had to be constantly alert. Those sharp horns and powerful hooves could be deadly, even if you weren't a clueless tourist.

At last it was time to go, but on our way back to the car I had a final conversation with a park ranger who seemed to be enjoying the corral antics as much as I was. "Do the bison have individual personalities?" I asked her. "And can you pick out individuals in the herd? They all look pretty similar to me."

"Oh, yes," she said. "The herdsmen who work with them regularly get to know them quite well. Some are easygoing and some are pretty hard to work with. And the old bulls, the ones isolated from the rest of the herd—well, those are the ones you really don't want to tangle with. We try to leave them alone as much as possible. They've earned their retirement."

The ranger went on to say that one animal in particular has captured the hearts of the park staff, a cow that was badly burned in a prairie fire several years ago. They weren't certain she'd survive her extensive injuries, but not only has she lived, but she has gone on to give birth. "She's a favorite of the staff," said the ranger. "She's easy to spot in the herd because of her scars."

The story brought tears to my eyes once again. I thought of the hollowed-out redwoods I'd seen in California, the ones who'd given me the message not to be afraid of the fire. The buffalo here had a similar message. Like the redwoods, they'd been victims of thoughtlessness and greed and cruelty. But they are also survivors, and with each new calf that's born in Custer State Park, the future of this sacred species is a little more secure in a world that almost lost them.

Fairbanks, Alaska, is one of the best places in the world to see the northern lights. (Photo credit: Bob Sessions)

9

Lights: The Northern Lights in Alaska

It's 3 a.m. in Fairbanks, Alaska, and I've been getting up every half hour since midnight, sleeping in fits and starts on the living room couch in the cabin Bob and I have rented on the outskirts of the city. I groan each time the alarm on my phone goes off, giving a resentful glance at the stairs that lead to the second floor where Bob is sleeping. Groggy with lack of sleep, I pull on my down jacket and wool cap, lace up my boots, stuff my hands into heavy mittens, and head outdoors into the zero-degree weather, feeling like Ralphie's little brother in *A Christmas Story*. I hope I won't trip and fall down, because Bob might well find me in the morning, frozen spread-eagled in the snow.

I trudge outside into the darkness, my boots making crunching sounds on the snow-packed driveway, and head far enough away from the cabin that I can get an unobstructed view of the sky. The cold is bitter against my face, the only part of me that's exposed to the elements, but at least it dispels my grogginess. I look upward, preparing to be disappointed, as I've been for the past six times I've checked the skies that night. But then I see them—the northern lights, the object of my quest.

Great shimmering waves of green are rippling across the night sky, dancing across the tops of the pine trees that surround the cabin. I stand enraptured, the cold forgotten. I know I should go inside to wake up Bob so he can join me, but I selfishly keep the experience to myself, fearful that if I look away even for a moment the lights will disappear. For long minutes it's just the aurora borealis and me, joined in a communion of heaven and earth that makes me feel as if I'm part of the light's mysterious, ethereal dance.

Bob and I had left Iowa in early November, leaving behind a landscape still cloaked in brown. After a series of flights, we landed at the Fairbanks airport close to midnight. The ride to our airport hotel was chilly, even with the shuttle's heater going full blast, and I could feel the cold pressing against the windows. The abrupt change from late autumn to full-on winter was disorienting, a feeling that intensified when we woke up the next morning to a wonderland of pine trees flocked with snow and a brilliant blue sky. We clearly weren't in Iowa anymore.

I'd come to Alaska not only to see the northern lights but also to reconnect with a cousin whom I hadn't seen in many years. Our reunion was a bit self-serving on my part, because she lives in the town of North Pole near Fairbanks, which is one of the best places in the world to see the aurora. As I planned our trip, I began to see reconnecting with Debbie as part of the renewed spiritual quest I'd been on ever since my mother's death just before the beginning of the pandemic. I have few relatives left, and so my visit with Debbie, the daughter of my mother's only sister, took on greater significance than it would for those who come from a large clan. Other than a brief meeting at her mother's funeral fourteen years before, we hadn't spent any time together since she'd left Iowa at the age of eighteen. Not sure how our reunion would go, and also not wanting to overstay our welcome, we planned to spend three nights with her and her husband and three in a cabin outside of Fairbanks.

As Debbie and her husband, Butch, came across the hotel lobby to greet us that first morning, I recognized her immediately. She still has the same kind smile of her youth, and I was struck by how much she looks like her mother. She's probably thinking the same about me, I thought, as we gave each other hugs. She introduced Butch, and I introduced Bob, and then we got down to the business of reestablishing a relationship that had been dormant for five decades. On our drive to North Pole we sketched out our lives—kids, jobs, and other details of life, an overview that would be given greater depth in the days to come. We learned how the two had moved to Alaska several decades before when Butch was stationed at Eielson Air Force Base, where Debbie held a civilian position working in the base's child education program. The two grew to love Alaska, and after retiring from their jobs with the military they had moved to the town of North Pole.

"You either hate Alaska and leave as soon as you can, or you fall under its spell," said Debbie. "We love the friendliness and sense of adventure in the people here, and also the vastness of the landscape. The beauty and stillness make you feel connected to nature in a way that's hard to explain. Part of it is the harshness of the weather—you really earn each season, as we say in Alaska. Winters are hard, summers are short, and each season has its challenges. But the beauties are remarkable."

"Like the lights," I said.

"Oh, yes, the lights," Debbie replied. "I never grow tired of them, even after all these years."

"What's the forecast for tonight?" I asked. I knew that the Geophysical Institute at the University of Alaska-Fairbanks has an aurora tracker that predicts viewing conditions, though like a weather forecast the predictions are just educated guesses.

"An average chance for tonight, then improving over the next few days," said Debbie. "Hopefully you'll get some good viewing during your time here."

A short time later we reached North Pole, a town of about 2,100 that embraces its holiday identity with gusto. We passed streetlights painted like candy canes and drove by a forty-two-foot statue of Santa Claus that stands overlooking Santa Claus House, an emporium of Alaska-themed gifts and Christmas merchandise that Debbie said is the town's most popular tourist attraction. The nearby Antler Academy had an outdoor pen with several reindeer (none of which sported a red nose, unfortunately). After our driving tour we headed to Debbie and Butch's neighborhood on the outskirts of town, an area with houses tucked beneath tall pines. In the yard next to theirs, a brown horse looked at us with curiosity as we passed by.

"That's Holly," Debbie said. "She often gets out of her pen, so you might meet her wandering around the neighborhood if you go for a walk. And keep your eye out for moose. They like to hang out in the ravine behind our house."

I was smiling as we got out of the car, realizing I was already falling under Alaska's spell.

While you can occasionally see the aurora borealis from the northern parts of the continental United States, for consistent viewing you need to travel to the polar regions. Fairbanks, Alaska, is an ideal spot because it sits underneath the Aurora Oval, a ring-shaped region where aurora activity is highest. The North Pole (the actual pole, not the town where my cousin lives) wears the oval like a halo, though a slightly lopsided one because it hangs farther south on the North American side than it does in Europe and Asia.

Aurora season typically runs between mid-September and early April, with peak viewing from January through March. Fairbanks makes it easy for tourists to see the lights with amenities such as heated "aurorium" cabins with windows on the ceiling, overnight dog-sledding adventures, photography classes, tour companies that pick you up at your place of lodging and take you to remote areas for prime viewing, and hotels that offer wake-up calls when the northern lights are out. It's estimated that visitors who spend three winter nights in Fairbanks have a 90 percent chance of seeing the aurora. I figured that with six nights in the area, and nearly eighteen hours of darkness each day, our chances were very good.

We headed to bed early that first night, setting our alarm for the middle of the night when the forecast said the chances were best for seeing the aurora. Debbie and Butch had generously offered us the use of their car, and after pulling on our clothes we crept quietly into their garage and cautiously backed out into the darkness. Our destination was the nearby Chena Lake Recreation Area, a two-thousand-acre park whose wide-open skies and minimal light pollution offer prime aurora viewing. Once there we found a parking spot and headed up the steep slope of a dike that overlooks a frozen river. Scanning the sky, we could see a faint ripple of color on the northern horizon, a display that was slowly drifting closer.

"Oh, wow!" I said, jumping up and down to warm up as well as express my excitement. "It's the lights! We're seeing the northern lights! Can you believe we're here?!"

Bob, however, was distracted and frustrated. His camera equipment was cold, and his hands colder. He couldn't get his lens to focus, so every shot he took was blurry. As I was enjoying the approaching lights he was fussing and grumbling, which soon made me upset too. What followed was one of those brief but intense arguments that long-time married couples have, in which you each know what the other person is going to say and you can short-circuit a lot of the preliminaries. Our argumentative efficiency was also aided by the fact that it was extremely cold.

"Just put down your camera and look at the lights," I told Bob, my temper rising.

"I have to get this figured out!" he said. "I don't want this trip to be a waste."

"It won't be a waste just because you can't take pictures," I snapped.

By the time we'd finished arguing, the aurora lights had retreated, along with my good mood. The stars were brilliant above us, shining with a brightness I'd rarely experienced, but the cold was seeping into our bones and we knew the quixotic lights could return any minute, or stay away the entire night. With an exasperated sigh, I agreed to Bob's suggestion that we head back.

Though the next day we were a little groggy, our midnight marital spat was forgotten in our eagerness to explore the area with Debbie and Butch. We stopped at the Christmas House to buy some gifts—its sled-dog-themed ornaments were adorable—and had our picture taken with Santa, both the forty-two-foot one and a living incarnation inside the store. Then we headed into the snowy wilderness that surrounds the town of North Pole, with my cousin and her husband pointing out places where they've camped, hunted, fished, and hiked with their family through the years.

As the hours passed, Debbie and I realized we are kindred spirits, swapping stories and memories with increasing animation. I was touched when she told me about the final visit our mothers had with each other. The two of them hadn't always gotten along, but when Debbie's mother was dying, my mother came to visit and was kind and compassionate, stroking her hair and telling her how much she loved her. I was grateful that their last hours together had been so loving and peaceful—and thankful, too, to have one last story about my mother, because I'd thought my storehouse of memories would never have another addition.

On an afternoon walk at the Chena Lake Recreation Area our conversation grew even more lively as we began to trade stories about our mothers' respective quirks. We agreed that while we loved them, they also could drive us crazy. "One of the weirdest things about my mom was that she hated fresh air," I said.

"Mine too!" Debbie said.

"She kept the windows in her house closed all the time, no matter what the weather, so when Bob and I visited in the summer we'd sneak a window open in our bedroom after she went to sleep. Then one time she caught us at it and we got such a talking-to we never dared do it again."

"I can top that," Debbie said. "Butch and I did the same thing, until the time we came to visit and saw that our bedroom window was nailed shut."

Our shared laughter filled the air, and it wasn't until later I realized the irony of two daughters of fresh-air-phobic mothers bonding in the chill winds of Alaska.

AN UNPREDICTABLE GIFT

Given how spectacular the northern lights are, it's not surprising that many cultures around the polar regions have myths and stories about them. In Estonia it was believed they were magnificent horse-drawn carriages carrying heavenly guests to a party, while in Norse mythology the lights were the weaponry of the warrior women known as Valkyries riding across the skies. A Finnish myth says the lights are sparked by a creature known as a firefox, who runs so fast that its tail causes sparks to fly into the heavens. In Sweden the lights were traditionally regarded as portents of good news. (The opposite was true in southern Europe, whose residents saw the lights very rarely and viewed them as evil omens.) In China the lights might well have been part of the origin of the legends about dragons flying across the sky, and in Japan it's believed that children conceived under the aurora will have good fortune. Among the Inuit who live in the polar regions, the aurora is generally linked with the world of the dead. Some believe the lights are spirits entering the afterlife, whose way is lit by those who have already crossed over.

The aurora borealis—and its southern cousin the aurora australis—remained a scientific mystery until the early twentieth century, with at least two dozen competing theories trying to explain their origin. Norwegian scientist Kristian Birkeland was the troubled genius who finally solved the puzzle. Beginning in 1899 he organized several expeditions to the polar regions, where he and his men endured harsh and dangerous conditions while gathering data. He correlated his observations of the aurora with solar activity and postulated that the lights were the result of the sun's electrons hitting the earth's atmosphere, where they were then pulled by its magnetic fields to the poles. Though the idea was dismissed by the scientific establishment for decades, his hypothesis proved correct.

In *The Northern Lights: The True Story of the Man Who Unlocked the Secrets of the Aurora Borealis*, Lucy Jago writes of the reaction of Birkeland's crew when they first saw the aurora in northern Norway, a description that echoes the wonder of contemporary observers:

> On the eastern horizon the darkness was splitting to reveal a gentle, tremulous luminescence—just a sliver, a streak. One by one the men stood still on the summit and stared at the vision appearing before them. The streamer of light began to move toward them in a huge arc across the heavens, pulsating and writhing as it advanced. The streak became a pennant with points of light coursing down in parallel lines like the strings of a harp, attached at one end to heaven and the other to a sinuous curve of light as it crept from horizon to horizon. Then another bolt of the green-white light stretched out beside the first and both arced together. Even more wildly the strings were plucked and the shapes changed to the music—now curling, now forming great circles, then breaking again to roll away to join another arc of green-white light. No one spoke. The hairs on the backs of their necks stood up, as if awoken by static electricity. Birkeland understood for the first time why the Lights had defied neat explanation: they appeared not to belong to Earth but to space. Seemingly beyond human comprehension, they reached straight into the souls of those who witnessed them as an appearance of the angelic host or the Holy Spirit might do.

At the Museum of the North on the University of Alaska–Fairbanks campus, Bob and I learned how subsequent generations of scientists have built upon Kristian Birkeland's research. As he had theorized, the lights are the result of charged particles ejected from the sun, a solar wind that takes about three days to hit the earth's atmosphere. After being channeled to the polar regions by the planet's magnetic fields, the charged particles light up the gases in the upper atmosphere sixty to 150 miles above the earth (a chemical reaction similar to what happens in neon lights such as those on the Las Vegas Strip, almost as if the northern lights are a kind of galactic advertisement for our planet). Greenish-yellow is the aurora's most common color, but shades of yellow, violet, red, and blue are often seen as well. I was surprised to learn that the auroras form nearly identical patterns at the northern and southern poles, a fact that wasn't known until the development of satellite photography.

According to a museum guide I spoke to, even those well versed in their scientific explanation think that the lights have a magical, mysterious quality. "Part of what makes them so intriguing is that they're on their own schedule," she answered when I asked if she thought seeing them was a spiritual experience. "You can put yourself in the right spot at the right time, but you can't control when they appear or disappear, and they're never the same, no matter how many times you see them. They're a good lesson in being humble and patient. All you can do when you see them is just stand there, awestruck."

I looked at Bob, wordlessly. He shrugged and smiled. He was feeling better about his photography woes after speaking with a local photographer who leads northern lights workshops. When Bob called him on the phone to explain his dilemma, the man generously gave him some tips—another instance of the Alaskan generosity of spirit that Debbie had told us about.

As for Debbie, she said she didn't think much about the science behind the aurora. "I see them as a gift from God," she said. "They're one of the best parts of life in the North."

LESSONS IN LIGHT

On Sunday morning we attended church with Debbie and Butch at their Catholic parish, which is (of course) named after St. Nicholas. Instead of stained-glass windows behind the altar there are large, clear windows, so that as we worshiped we could see snowflakes drifting down. I was also charmed to see the many Alaskan motifs in the church's architecture and furnishings, including a lectern made from logs and a tabernacle (the small box that holds the body and blood of Christ in Catholic churches) in the form of a rustic cabin. It felt good to be back in a church again, I realized. Back in Iowa we'd returned to services as well, but we had so many COVID-19 precautions in place that there was an edge of anxiety in the air that I didn't sense here.

While the setting was thoroughly Alaskan, the priest was from a place about as far away as you can get from the polar region: Zimbabwe. In his sermon, the felicitously named Father Welcome talked about the need to care for widows and orphans and of his own mother's difficulties as a widow. "Many of them are very lonely and struggle to survive," he said in his accented English. It was good to be reminded of the biblical command to care for widows and orphans, which is so clear in the Gospels but is not often preached about in America, at least in my experience.

It all felt a little dreamlike, to be in North Pole watching the snow fall behind the altar, listening to a priest from Zimbabwe talk about widows and orphans in Africa. As I looked around the nearly full church I could see a range of ethnicities, a reflection of the diversity brought to the area by the Air Force and Army bases located nearby. And there we all were, worshiping together in a church dedicated to St. Nicholas.

My thoughts drifted to the aurora, wondering what its religious correlative would be. The redwoods had reminded me of cathedrals, the sandhill cranes of angels, and the hot springs of Oregon of baptism. But the northern lights? That stumped me, until my eyes lit on the snow visible through the altar windows. You don't need stained glass in Alaska, I thought, because nature is so impressive here. I imagined the dark sky of the Alaskan night as one immense stained-glass window, only with moving swirls that eclipse even the most stunning of cathedral windows. My earlier travels had made me ponder whether God might be a geologist, a mathematician, or an astronomer, but there was no doubt in my mind that he is also an artist, because the evidence for the divine love of beauty is everywhere.

I knew a little about stained glass from my travels in Europe, where I'd marveled at the artistry of windows in churches such as St. Paul's in London, Chartres Cathedral in France, and St. Stephen's in Vienna. Stained glass developed into a major art form during the Middle Ages, when architectural and technical innovations allowed the builders of cathedrals to include great tapestries of colored glass in their designs. The windows reinforced communal beliefs and helped teach biblical stories to the largely illiterate people who sat in the pews. But they had a powerful emotional effect as well, one that is still felt by modern pilgrims. The windows pierce the somber interiors of churches with shafts of colored light, emphasizing the fact that this is sacred space. And though the windows are static, their light shifts with the time of day and the season, creating slow-motion versions of the aurora on a winter night.

According to religious art scholar Virginia Chieffo Raguin, medieval theologians regarded creation as a process of emanations of divine light, from the "first radiance" of Christ down to the lowliest speck of matter. "In order to ascend from the lowest to the highest, one searches for the trace of divine light in all creatures," she writes in *The History of Stained Glass: The Art of Light, Medieval to Contemporary.* "Light was transparent as it left the Creator, acquiring colour, and thus its ability to be visible, as it penetrated the material world. Colours can therefore be seen as representing the diversity and imperfection of creatures, although they still betray the radiance of their origins."

Light dazzles in other religions too. One of the best examples is Diwali, a joyous festival for Hindus, Sikhs, and Jains that celebrates the triumph of light over darkness and good over evil. In Judaism, the eight-day celebration of Hanukkah commemorates the rededication of the Second Temple in Jerusalem in 161 BCE, when a lamp miraculously burned for eight days until new consecrated oil could be found. In remembrance, the multibranched candelabra known as a menorah is lit each evening.

As I thought more about the spirituality of light, I realized I had a connection much closer to home thanks to Bob's passion for photography. From him I've learned to appreciate the beauty of the golden hour, that time at dawn and dusk when the light often takes on a shimmering quality, sometimes bathing the entire landscape in shades of gold. "At times like that the light does the work for you," Bob says. "You just have to show up."

Even aside from the golden hour, at any time of the day light makes the difference between an ordinary photo and an exceptional one. I've often been surprised to see what Bob is able to capture on his camera by focusing on some detail that's illuminated by the light, from the ripples on a pond to the speckled pattern of a leaf. He's made me realize that those of us who live in more southern latitudes than Alaska have our own, more subtle, version of the aurora—one that exists on earth, rather than in the heavens.

REVEALED IN DARKNESS

When we left Debbie and Butch's house to stay in our rented cabin near Fairbanks, we made plans to meet again on our last evening in the city, grateful for the friendship that had sprung up among the four of us. While I wasn't eager to leave them, our time on our own had the advantage of allowing me to focus even more obsessively on the lights. Over the next days Bob and I became increasingly sleep deprived, our nights disrupted and our waking hours fueled by multiple cups of coffee. The trip began to take on a surreal cast, a disorienting mix of long nights and brilliantly sunny days, all linked by the aurora's ribbons of light.

During our explorations in the area we met a number of fellow travelers who were there to see the lights, including a family from Los Angeles and a honeymooning couple from Japan.

Many of the locals also hailed from other parts of the world, though they seemed so well adapted to the region they may as well have been natives. One was a volunteer guide at Creamer's Field Migratory Waterfowl Refuge, a burly man who led a nature hike one afternoon. When he showed up at the visitor center to meet us, I was disappointed to see his sweat pants, tennis shoes, and lightweight coat, an outfit at odds with the ten-degree cold. Well, this is likely to be a short walk, I thought with disappointment.

I couldn't have been more wrong. Despite having bad knees and being dressed for fifty-degree weather, the man was indefatigable. As we explored the warren of trails at the refuge, he gave us a cornucopia of information about the ecology of the region. I soon gave up asking questions because every time I did, he stopped his already slow pace to answer them in detail, during which time my inner temperature dropped a notch lower. Bob, in contrast, kept peppering him with queries, his fascination with the landscape insulating him from the cold.

"Now we haven't talked much about moose yet, have we?" the guide asked after nearly two hours, stopping yet again on the snowy trail as he began another mini-lecture. "They're incredibly well adapted to winter. Wildlife biologists have tried to figure out at what point moose have to increase their metabolism to deal with the cold. They've tested them down to twenty below and they still haven't turned up their thermostats."

Bob asked a follow-up question, despite me mouthing "No" and frantically shaking my head behind the guide's back. For whatever reason, his marital radar was offline. By now I was so cold I could barely feel my feet.

"That's really interesting, but I need to warm up," I interrupted. "Which direction is the visitor center?"

The man looked at me in surprise. "You're cold?"

"I'm freezing."

"Take that turn over there and follow the signs," he said kindly, obviously thinking that Iowans are made of weak stock. As I raced away, I could hear him starting a disquisition on the mating habits of moose.

On two of our last three nights in the area, we got lucky. Bundled up against the subzero cold, we had multiple sightings of the northern lights, each display different from the next. They'd appear and disappear on their own schedule, shimmering curtains of yellow-green tinged with pink that rippled across the sky. My neck grew tired from gazing upward, and Bob's hands were nearly frozen from manipulating his camera, but I had my fill of beauty and Bob got some wonderful photos.

As the week went on, I found myself thinking about a paradox that the northern lights had revealed to me: in order to appreciate light, we need darkness. The aurora is a grand testimony to this truth, because while the sun's magnetic particles are drifting toward earth all the time, it's only at night that their interactions with gasses in the upper atmosphere are visible. On a more earthbound level, during the day thousands of objects grab our visual attention every waking minute, but in the darkness we can see what is normally hidden. The human eye is so sensitive that at night we can spot a candle flame at a distance of two miles, for example, as well as stars that are thousands of light-years from Earth.

That's part of why the modern world's relentless drive to get rid of darkness is a problem. Around the world, true darkness is disappearing as cities and towns light their streets at ever-greater illumination levels. Even in rural areas, many households have yard lights that flip on as soon as evening falls. As a result, more than one-third of humans live in areas where they can't see the Milky Way, including nearly 80 percent of North Americans. While the spread of artificial light has many negative consequences for the natural world, including nocturnal animals who are more vulnerable to predators, and birds whose migratory patterns are disrupted, we humans suffer as well. We've evolved over millennia to spend significant time in darkness, and being bathed in artificial light for much of our lives has wide-ranging effects on our health.

Our negative attitude toward darkness also has spiritual implications, writes Barbara Brown Taylor in her book *Learning to Walk in the Dark*. In Christian and Jewish thought, light is almost always good, and darkness is usually bad. "God is light and in him there is no darkness at all," as a New Testament epistle puts it (1 John 1:5). Taylor points out that the dualistic language of popular theology often sets up opposites: good/ evil, church/world, spirit/flesh, and light/dark. The second of those pairings is always lesser than the first, with one close to God and the other farther away. But it's clear from the Bible that God works in the darkness as well as in the light, from the story of Jacob wrestling with a divine being in the night to the prophetic dreams of Joseph in Egypt. In our own lives, our dark nights of the soul can teach us more about divine mysteries than years of attending church services. As Taylor writes, "I have learned things in the dark that I could never have learned in the light, things that have saved my life over and over again, so that there is really only one logical conclusion. I need darkness as much as I need light."

I remembered Debbie saying that she appreciated how the Alaskan winter is a time of rest and renewal after the high energy of the summer when the sun hardly sets. I thought, too, of ancient people entering sacred places such as Dunbar Cave in Tennessee, descending into the darkness in hopes of touching the divine, and of the pandemic, whose cloud of suffering had revealed things that were hidden. Darkness, both figurative and literal, can help us see with new clarity.

The day before we left Alaska, Bob and I had a conversation with a woman who works in a vodka distillery in Fairbanks, where we stopped for cocktails one afternoon. (On my trips, spiritual research takes many forms.) When the woman heard we were from Iowa, her face lit up. "I love Iowa!" she said, and told of coming to our home state for reunions of a cross-country peace march she'd participated in a number of years ago.

When I asked how she'd ended up in Fairbanks, she said she was a Boston native who'd moved to the state a couple of years ago because she wanted to get to know its landscape. She loves Fairbanks in large part because of its residents. "People come here from all over," she said. "Some are in the military, and some work on the pipeline. There are hunters and back-to-the-land environmentalists. You wouldn't think we'd all get along, but we do. I think it's because the climate is so harsh here. You know you need to have good neighbors in case something goes wrong. If your car breaks down on the highway, you've got five people stopping in the first ten minutes to make sure you're all right."

She added that the aurora is one of her favorite parts of living in Alaska and said that she'll text her friends in the middle of the night when the lights are especially vibrant. "The lights are always different, and they always lift my spirits," she said.

I came away from that conversation—and from Alaska—with a renewed sense of optimism. Maybe we're going to be OK, I thought, despite the pandemic and all the troubles of the world. If North Pole, Alaska, can have a beloved priest from Zimbabwe, and peace marchers from Boston can live in harmony with Alaskan hunters and pipeline workers, maybe some of the fractures in our larger society can heal too. It's easy to forget how dependent we are on each other in the lower forty-eight states, but even if our temperatures don't get to forty below our lives are still intertwined. Maybe Alaskans have a better sense for that in part because of their shared wonder at the aurora.

Our flight out of Fairbanks left in the middle of the night. I peered out of the plane's window, searching for one last view of the northern lights. Though they didn't cooperate in bidding me farewell, it comforted me to know they would return to the Alaskan skies on their own mysterious schedule. Whether they're formed by the solar wind, a firefox racing across the snow, or ancestors looking down on their descendants, the lights are a gift. As we flew into the darkness, I imagined my mother and aunt, those two women so determined to keep their windows closed, now dancing with the northern lights across the sky. I hoped they were pleased at the connection forged between their daughters, way down below them in the cold of an Alaskan winter.

At the Kīlauea crater in Hawai'i Volcanoes National Park, a lake of fire mesmerizes visitors. (PHOTO CREDIT: BOB SESSIONS)

10

Fire: Hawai'i Volcanoes National Park

Beginning in the third century, a group of Christians known as the Desert Fathers and Mothers fled to the Egyptian desert to escape the temptations of the world and devote themselves to God. The stories about them are often profound, sometimes confusing, and at other times just plain weird. Take the tale of a zealous monk who sought advice from an older monk who was renowned for his wisdom. The younger man said to the elder, "Father, I follow the rules and fast, pray, and meditate. I do my best to purify my thoughts. Now what more should I do?"

In reply the old man stood up and stretched out his hands to heaven, and as he did so his fingers became ten lamps of fire. He answered, "Why not become fire?"

Well, that's a doozy of a response. Did his hands really burst into flames? What did he mean by "becoming fire"? Who knows? All I can say is that I love the contrast between the earnest, good-boy approach of the supplicant and the over-the-top response of a man whose soul had been seared in the spiritual fire of the desert. Quit trying to follow all the rules, son. Try bursting into flames instead.

When I was thinking of a trip to explore the concept of sacred fire, I took this story as my guide. Fire called for something extravagant, an experience that would balance the austere beauties of Alaska's northern lights. I'd experienced the power of fire before, of course, from campfires and candles to fireworks. But to truly experience the element of fire I wanted something more intense—which is why I planned a trip to Hawai'i Volcanoes National Park, where I hoped to gaze into the fiery bowels of the earth.

As in Alaska, I was fortunate to have a personal connection to this destination. Our friends Jennifer and Kirk had recently moved to Hawai'i, where Jennifer had taken a position as vicar of an Episcopal church.

"Aren't you worried about becoming a vicar?" I asked when she accepted the job in Kapa'au, a small town on the north end of the Big Island. "They do seem to meet terrible ends in mystery novels. Poisoned in pubs, drowned in moats, stabbed at afternoon teas—that sort of thing happens all the time."

Jennifer assured me that she'd take proper safety precautions in her new job, and her glowing reports of their new lives in Hawai'i made me eager to visit, especially after the temperatures began to plunge in Iowa. By January Bob and I could hardly wait to escape the snow and ice of a midwestern winter. While some of our friends had questioned our sanity in traveling to Alaska in November, no one was surprised we wanted to visit Hawai'i in January.

Swapping ten degrees for seventy-five, we landed in the Kona Airport on the Big Island, where the fragrant smells of tropical vegetation and warm air caressed our senses as soon as we stepped out of the plane. An hour's drive through rural countryside brought us to Jennifer and Kirk's house, where we strolled through their yard filled with fruit trees, ferns, and thick foliage. Amid the lush beauty, though, we were puzzled by some deep gashes in one part of the lawn.

"Feral pigs," Kirk explained. "They're common in this part of the island."

"Could be worse—think of all those mystery novels," I said, raising my eyebrows at Jennifer, who grinned.

While in Alaska we'd worshiped at St. Nicholas Church amid falling snow, in Hawai'i we attended St. Augustine's, a historic, wooden-frame church that sits atop a hill crowned by palm trees. Founded as a mission of the Church of England in 1884 by English families who immigrated to Hawai'i because of the sugar cane industry, through the years St. Augustine's has been home to a diverse congregation, with parishioners of Japanese, Chinese, Filipino, Portuguese, Puerto Rican, Korean, African, Hawaiian, Samoan, and European ancestry. As in North Pole, it was a little disorienting to be in a church so similar and yet so different from what I was accustomed to. Hawaiian elements were threaded through its liturgy and music, with the melodious syllables of the Hawaiian language as soothing as the gentle breezes that wafted through the open windows.

After the service we visited with parishioners, who asked us about the plans for our stay on the island. When we said we were headed to Volcanoes National Park, we were told to bring a gift for Pele, the volcano goddess who lives there. "You want to stay on Pele's good side," explained a woman. "And don't take any rocks with you when you leave—that makes her angry. Every year hundreds of tourists send rocks back to Hawai'i because they think they're bringing them bad luck."

A respect for Pele was just one of the beliefs of *Kanaka Maoli* (native Hawaiians) we encountered among the people we met through Jennifer and Kirk, who were learning alongside us as newcomers to the island. Especially intriguing was the widespread recognition that certain spots on the island are places of *mana*, or spiritual power. Some are associated with significant events in Hawai'i's history, including the birthplace near Kapa'au of King Kamehameha the Great, a powerful and complex leader who conquered the islands in 1810. Others are the site of *heiau*, sacred temples built by ancient Hawaiians, the remains of which can still be seen in various locations across the islands. "The *heiau* are considered living spiritual temples, and you need to enter these places with respect," said Jennifer, whose parishioners have taken her to several of those sacred sites. "And some of them you shouldn't approach at all unless you have permission from those who still watch over them."

We learned more about native beliefs at Puʻuhonua o Hōnaunau National Historical Park, which preserves one of the most sacred sites in Hawaiʻi. Located on a pristine stretch of coastline south of Kona, Puʻuhonua o Hōnaunau is deeply rooted in the ancient traditions of the islands. Its visitor center describes how Polynesians who likely came from the Marquesas Islands arrived in the archipelago more than fifteen hundred years ago in canoes carrying plants, animals, and supplies. The new residents of Hawaiʻi believed in an array of gods, goddesses, spirits, and guardian ancestors and developed a system of laws called *kapu*, a word meaning "forbidden" or "sacred" (the English *taboo* derives from *kapu*). Some of the rules helped preserve the ecological balance of the islands, including restrictions on which fish could be caught in which season, while others enforced strict social hierarchies, such as prohibitions against commoners looking directly upon chiefs or even stepping in their shadows. Many additional *kapu* laws governed daily life in matters large and small. Men and women were not allowed to dine together, for example, and women were forbidden to eat bananas, pork, taro, and coconuts. Breaking one of these rules, even without meaning to, was punishable by death.

Puʻuhonua o Hōnaunau had great spiritual power because it was a royal enclosure, a burial site of chiefs, and a place of refuge for those who had broken the *kapu* laws. If people reached this spot—which wasn't easy, because it was sandwiched between a great wall and a shoreline of sharp rocks—they could receive absolution from priests and escape being killed. In times of war, defeated warriors and their families sought sanctuary here as well.

Although the islands had other places of refuge for *kapu* breakers, Puʻuhonua o Hōnaunau is the best preserved and has the most dramatic setting. King Kamehameha ended the *kapu* system in 1819, and the bones of chiefs have been removed, but it's still a place of beauty and sacredness. Carved wooden figures representing various Hawaiian gods stand on its coastline, their stern expressions warning visitors to treat this sanctuary with respect.

I was happy to follow their command as I wandered the grounds in brilliant sunshine, hearing the rhythmic pulse of the nearby waves and the singing of birds in the palm trees overhead. This was a place for second chances, I realized—something that any religion worth its salt provides. I thought, too, of how traces of traditional Hawaiian beliefs had surfaced in my conversations with residents of the island. Their admonitions against taking rocks from the island and warnings to be careful around places of power had more than a hint of *kapu* about them. Hawai'i has kept its ties to the elemental forces of its sacred land better than any other place I've traveled. Tourists come here for the beaches, sun, and surf, not realizing that these islands have deeper lessons to teach them.

FIRE AS RESURRECTION

Hawai'i wouldn't exist without the bubbling cauldrons of fire beneath it, because the entire chain of islands is comprised of land formed by lava flowing from underwater volcanoes. Over millions of years the barren rock was slowly transformed into mineral-rich soil in which wind-blown seeds flourished, eventually creating the lush tropical paradise of today. The land-building process continues: in thousands of years a subterranean volcano named Lo'ihi is expected to reach the surface, where it will create either an entirely new island or an extension of the Big Island, depending upon how the lava flows.

The supernatural entity who gets credit for this is Pele, the Hawaiian goddess of volcanoes and fire. It's said that Pele arrived in Hawai'i from Tahiti in a canoe provided by her brother, the god of sharks. She was going to marry the fire god Aila'au, but her tempestuous reputation preceded her and he fled. After traveling the length of the islands she found a home in the crater of the Kīlauea volcano. Her full name is Pelehonuamea, "She who shapes the sacred land," but she has other titles depending upon her mood. When she erupts, she's known as *ka wahine o ka lua*, the woman of the pit. When lava flows, she's *ka wahine 'ai honua*, the eater of the land.

Before the coming of Christianity, Pele was one of the most revered of all the gods, and she continues to be honored to this day. Many native Hawaiians consider her part of their *'ohana* or family. They believe she can take different guises, including that of an old woman who wanders the islands testing people's kindness. If you treat her well, she will bless you; if not, watch out. Even the National Park Service pays homage to her on the website for Volcanoes National Park: "The presence of Pelehonuamea is not necessarily approached with fear, but with respect. . . . In Hawaiian tradition, it is customary to ask permission from Pele to travel through her land and this sacred landscape."

Fire plays a prominent role in spiritual traditions around the globe. Pele is one of many fire deities, from Morimi, the Yoruba goddess of fire, to the Egyptian sun god Ra. The ancient Romans believed that as long as a flame burned in the Temple of Vesta the city of Rome would endure, while the Greeks told the story of how the god Prometheus gave the gift of fire to humanity, which made Zeus so angry that he sentenced Prometheus to have his liver torn out by an eagle each day. And as I recounted earlier, sometimes the old fire gods got recycled into new ones, as when the Celtic pagan Brigid became St. Brigid.

In Judaism and Christianity, fire is among the most powerful of spiritual metaphors, one that God has used liberally through the millennia. Think of Moses encountering God in a burning bush or of the pillar of fire that guided the Israelites in their wanderings through the desert. The prophet Malachi said that God is like a silversmith who purifies our hearts in a refining fire that burns away the dross. At Pentecost, tongues of fire—or something that resembled them—appeared above the heads of Jesus' followers. Fire is an essential part of many church rituals to this day, from the candles burning on the altar during Sunday services to the fires lit on Easter morning to symbolize resurrection. In Judaism, meanwhile, the lighting of candles heralds the beginning of Shabbat each Friday evening, a ritual accompanied by the reciting of an ancient Hebrew blessing: "Blessed are You, Eternal our God, Sovereign of time and space. You hallow us with Your mitzvot and command us to kindle the lights of Shabbat."

While Earth is a water planet, you can make an equally good argument that it's defined by fire, because while the gaseous planets in our solar system have lightning, none have the necessary elements for true fire. "Earth alone holds fire," writes Stephen J. Pyne in *The Pyrocene: How We Created an Age of Fire, and What Happens Next.* "It's worth pausing over this remarkable circumstance. Among planets fire is as rare as life, and for the same reason: fire on Earth is a creation of the living world. Life in the oceans gave Earth an oxygen atmosphere. Life on land gave Earth combustible hydrocarbons. As soon as plants rooted on land, lightning set them ablaze. They've been burning ever since."

Pyne explains that while fire isn't alive in the conventional sense, life called it into being and sustains it. Fire feeds on biomass and spreads by the contagion of combustion, deconstructing with one hand and reassembling with the other—a kind of shake and bake that stirs molecules, organisms, and landscapes, rewiring the flow of energy and nutrients. Scientists have only recently come to appreciate the complex and crucial role it plays in many ecosystems, and as a result a growing number of locales are moving away from the impossible goal of suppressing fires and instead are trying to manage them. "The more we try to remove fire from places that have coevolved with it, the more violently fire will return," writes Pyne.

Peering back into the origin of our species, fire made us human. The ability to kindle and manipulate it set us apart from other animals and set in motion revolutions in food, energy, shelter, and toolmaking. Because cooked foods are more nutritious and easier to digest than raw ones, our brains grew larger and our cultural and social development flourished. Instead of spending a good share of each day chewing food like our primate cousins do, our early ancestors grilled meat over campfires, ate in a hurry, and had plenty of time for other activities. Fire also protected them from the cold, greatly increasing the range of climates they could inhabit. They learned how to burn grasslands to make them more productive for grazing animals and how to fire clay into pottery to store food and water. And fire encouraged communal bonds, from the gathering of firewood to the tending of the hearth.

That third-century monk in the desert told his disciple to become fire, but in one sense we already are; our bodies are fueled by the fire of our metabolism. This internal fire grows and repairs our cells, moves our limbs, inflates our lungs, circulates our blood, and powers all the other processes that enable us to live. Most of the time it works without us being aware of it, until something throws it off balance. I remember when Bob was in the hospital with ehrlichiosis, a tick-borne bacterial illness that's difficult to diagnose. The medical staff put ice packs around his body to help bring down his high fever, using the oldest of remedies amid the high-tech paraphernalia of the intensive care unit. Bob fully recovered, thank goodness, but I'll never forget the experience of sitting by his side and sensing the fire that blazed through his body, the equivalent of a forest fire raging out of control.

I've had the opposite experience, too, of watching that inner fire fade at the bedside of those who are dying. Instead of burning too hot, their inner flames grow weaker, gradually declining in intensity as their feet begin to grow mottled and their hands become cold. The body instinctively conserves its heat as it enters its final stage, drawing energy away from extremities in a futile effort to save its vital organs. At last the flame of life that had been kindled at birth flickers out, a candle blown out by a puff of breath from the Great Beyond.

My time in Hawai'i contemplating fire made me remember a prairie burn I'd watched the year before, not long after the beginning of COVID-19. When friends who owned the prairie invited me to watch, I'd eagerly accepted, both because it was something to relieve the monotony of quarantine and because I knew that a grassland fire is one of the Midwest's best shows. Fires like this are essential for prairies, an endangered ecosystem that once covered much of the Great Plains. Prairie fires kill invasive species, release nutrients into the soil, remove the dry thatch of previous growth, and allow the native plants to flourish. And they're a guilt-free way to enjoy the drama of a huge fire.

The burn didn't disappoint. I stood as close as the professional fire-tenders allowed, entranced by ten-foot-high flames leaping and dancing as crackling sounds filled the air and blasts of intense heat pulsated from the burning grasses. I'd seen prairie burns before, but none as large as this one. It seemed as if all the sunshine that had nourished these plants for years was being released in one intense, brief conflagration, flinging back to the universe all that stored-up energy.

Appropriately, the burn happened on Good Friday. During that peculiar Holy Week in the first months of the pandemic, the fire seemed an all-too-apt metaphor for the disease, death, economic disruption, and political unrest that were spreading through the world. Watching the flames, I realized this was the most memorable Good Friday I'd ever experienced, a liturgy enacted by fire and wind and grass, with death and life intertwining in an ecstatic release of energy. I knew that in the coming weeks tiny green shoots would appear in this blackened field, newly fertilized and bursting with life. They will have their time in the sun over the next few years, until it's time for another prairie burn, and then the whole cycle will begin again. A parable of resurrection indeed.

As Annie Dillard writes in *Pilgrim at Tinker Creek*:

If the landscape reveals one certainty, it is that the extravagant gesture is the very stuff of creation. After the one extravagant gesture of creation in the first place, the universe has continued to deal exclusively in extravagances, flinging intricacies and colossi down aeons of emptiness, heaping profusions on profligacies with ever-fresh vigor. The whole show has been on fire from the word go. I come down to the water to cool my eyes. But everywhere I look I see fire; that which isn't flint is tinder, and the whole world sparks and flames.

SHE WHO SHAPES THE SACRED LAND

At first Bob thought I was kidding when I told him he couldn't take any rocks from the island. "Really?" he asked. "Not even a small one?"

"Not even a small one," I repeated.

Fortunately, Jennifer and Kirk seconded my opinion about the foolishness of risking the ire of Pele. The four of us were in a car on our way to Volcanoes National Park on the southern end of the Big Island, a trip that would be the culmination of our stay in Hawai'i. "That rule against picking up rocks, wood, shells, or coral is an important part of showing respect for the land and keeping things in their natural place," Jennifer said. "Many people observe it as part of a widespread sense that this land is sacred and needs to be protected."

As we drove, we got an overview of the Big Island's impressive ecological diversity, which includes four out of the world's five major climate types, from fertile pastures where cattle graze to tropical forests that get more than 200 inches of rain a year and semi-arid uplands that look like Wyoming. Snow-capped Mauna Kea provided a scenic background for much of our route. The top of the island's tallest mountain is home to an array of international research facilities and observatories, which Kirk pointed out as we drove.

"The Big Island works hard to minimize light pollution to help the astronomers working at the top of Mauna Kea," he explained. "I'm not the only one who finds the dark skies to be one of the most remarkable things about the Big Island. When we moved here, we were surprised at how dark the roads are at night, how few street lights the towns have, and how many stars we can see."

After checking into our lodging in a town on the outskirts of Volcanoes National Park, we started exploring its 333,000 acres, which include two active volcanoes. Mauna Loa is the earth's most massive mountain, so big it actually bends the ocean floor beneath it. If you include the part that's underwater, it stands at 56,000 feet, a full 27,000 feet taller than Mt. Everest. The other mountain is Kīlauea, one of the world's most active volcanoes, which has been erupting almost continuously since 1983. Unlike explosive volcanoes that blow their tops with devastating consequences, Kīlauea and Mauna Loa are more like simmering pots that periodically bubble over with rivers of lava. You don't want to get caught in the path of the molten rock, but you're not likely to be blown skyward.

A stop at the visitor center provided us with an overview of the park, which is both an International Biosphere Reserve and UNESCO World Heritage Site. "This is an island within an island," a ranger told us in a presentation on the park's efforts to eradicate invasive species and reintroduce native ones. Feral pigs and mongoose are on the undesirable list, for example, as well as nonnative plants such as Himalayan ginger and fire tree. About 90 percent of Hawai'i's native flora is found nowhere else on earth, having evolved in the isolation of the Hawaiian archipelago. You have to admire the tenacity of the species that originally colonized these barren rocks. It's estimated that winds and sea currents deposited new species at the rate of one insect every 68,000 years, one plant every 98,000 years, and one bird every million years. Hearing those statistics made me appreciate the beauty of Hawai'i even more.

A hike on the 3.3-mile Kīlauea Iki Trail gave us an up-close view of the power of a volcano. After walking through rainforest, we descended into a bowl-shaped crater left behind by a 1959 eruption. The former lava lake is now a desolate expanse of broken and uneven rocks with a few small plants growing in their cracks, the first stage of a regeneration process that after a thousand years or so will result in a rainforest. At the other end of the crater, the trail led us upward into greenery once again, where we explored a lava tube, a hollowed-out cave formed from molten rock five centuries ago.

We saw more evidence of volcanic power as we drove the park's Chain of Craters Road, an eighteen-mile route that descends to the coast and ends at a 2003 lava flow that extends far into the ocean. Since 1983, more than 875 acres of new land have been added to the Big Island, though it's going to be a long time before anyone is going to build homes there.

As impressive as these sites are, the true superstar of the park is the lava lake in the Kīlauea crater, which is where we headed next. This is one of the few places on the planet where ordinary people, not just volcanologists, can get relatively close to an active volcano. Park officials and geologists constantly monitor its status to make certain it's safe to observe from a distance (though if you have respiratory issues it's best to stay away, as the gasses emanating from the crater can cause difficulties).

To reach the crater overlook we hiked about a mile across a blasted landscape reminiscent of Mordor in *The Lord of the Rings*. The bleak views sobered my mood, making me better understand the very real destructive power of a volcano. Even a relatively benign one like Kīlauea is capable of great damage, as when more than seven hundred houses were destroyed in a 2018 eruption. It's no wonder, I thought, that the ancient Hawaiians came to believe that a divine being resides here. How else could you explain the tremendous power that simmers below the surface of this mountain?

As we drew closer we saw steam rising into the air and smelled sulphur in the wind. We came over a hill and saw the lava lake about a half mile away, a boiling mix of fire and broken rock that bubbled like a massive cauldron stirred by giants. The viewing area was cordoned off with ropes that kept us from venturing farther, though I wasn't even tempted to draw closer to the dangerous lake. Remembering the admonition to bring a gift for Pele, I'd purchased some flowers at the outskirts of the park, and I placed them on the ground next to several other flowers just outside of the safety rope, seeing that I wasn't the only person who wanted to stay on Pele's good side. If this is her home, she's one tough goddess indeed.

I thought of what prayer to offer a fire goddess. Perhaps for cleansing, or for illumination? Or maybe just to be left alone? I wondered what the Desert Father would do here, the one who'd advised the younger monk to become fire. Mystics in many traditions have that same attraction to fire, often advising their devotees to take a metaphorical dive into the flames. As a water person, I'd much rather dive into a clear, cool lake of good old-fashioned H_2O, but being at the edge of the volcano gave me a visceral sense for the magnetic pull of fire.

In Christianity, fire evokes both the Holy Spirit and the flames of hell, proof of the contradictory nature of this element. In Buddhism, the Buddha's Fire Sermon is one of his most famous discourses, a cautionary tale delivered to an audience of fire-worshiping ascetics. Be careful, the Buddha said, because the eyes, ears, tongue, body, and mind all feed the fires of lust, anger, sorrow, desire, and delusion. His words were so convincing that the ascetics all attained instant enlightenment.

In short, fire is nothing to play around with. Even a candle burning on a winter's night—a tiny cousin of the lava lake in front of me—carries a hint of danger. "Be sure to blow it out before you go to bed," Bob will warn as he heads upstairs to bed, repeating a timeless admonition. Fire requires care, no matter what form it takes.

The next morning we got up at 4:30, hoping to see Kīlauea's lava lake once again, this time framed by darkness. After parking our car, we headed out on the trail with flashlights, a repeat of the walk we'd taken the afternoon before. This time the route seemed even more solemn and significant. We could see a reddish glow in the distance, a light that grew larger and brighter as we approached. Choosing our steps carefully, at last we came to the point where we could see the lake of fire in its full glory, a view dramatically enhanced by the lack of light.

Yellow, orange, and red streams of lava spurted upward and then crashed back into the lake, where slabs of broken rock and huge clots of incandescent fire swirled and bubbled.

A crowd of about twenty people stood quietly in the viewing area. Some took pictures, but most of us watched in silence, mesmerized by the otherworldly scene. It felt as if we were witnessing something primal, almost as if we were present at the beginning of time. Thinking of the images of Pele that I'd seen at the park's art gallery, many depicting her with locks of fire and skin that glowed from within, I felt an involuntary shiver. Destruction is necessary for life, she seemed to be saying, a similar message to those given by the redwoods and the buffalo. Don't fear the fire. Embrace it.

We stood for a long time, watching as dawn crept over the horizon, and then the lake's splendor gradually faded in the sunlight, like a fierce animal settling down for a nap.

An hour later we left the park, starting our drive back to the airport from which Bob and I would fly out later that day. As we drove, Jennifer checked her phone for messages. "Well, this is appropriate," she said. "I just got an email telling me that today is St. Brigid's Day. She's an Irish saint who's connected to the pre-Christian goddess of fire. Do you know of her?"

"Oh, yes, I do," I said, feeling a shiver run up my arms once again.

I'd gotten this same message at many holy sites around the world: everything is connected. Pele and Brigid, life and death, light and darkness, creation and destruction. I thought of my mother's body, purified in the flame of a crematorium, and her ashes that had provided the impetus for a cross-country pilgrimage that had taken me to far-flung sites across a continent. And there was the flame of the pandemic too, which still blazed in many parts of the world. Much was being destroyed, but if my time with Pele had taught me anything, it's that the seeds of new life can sprout in even the most devastated of landscapes.

As we drove away from Kīlauea, I knew I'd never look at the flickering flame of a candle in the same way again.

Chaco Culture National Historical Park preserves a complex of massive buildings constructed by the Ancestral Puebloan people between 850 and 1250 CE. (Photo credit: Bob Sessions)

11

Astronomy: Chaco Canyon in New Mexico

If you're planning to visit Chaco Canyon in northwestern New Mexico, be prepared for The Road. Reaching the national park—officially known as Chaco Culture National Historical Park—requires driving for about an hour on a route that the National Park Service euphemistically describes as "rough." Full of ruts, rocks, and washouts, the unpaved road will wreak havoc on your car's suspension system unless you creep along at just a few miles an hour. If it's recently rained, the route is nearly impassable. But for many of those who love Chaco Canyon, The Road is fine just the way it is, bone-rattling wash-boards and all. If you want to get to Chaco, you're going to have to work for it.

Even after you arrive in Chaco, the park is far from hospitable. It has no gas stations, repair services, or food vendors, and its only lodging is a small campground with no showers. Set in a high, semi-desert valley between sandstone canyon walls, it averages just eight inches of rain a year. In winter the temperature plunges below freezing many nights, while in summer the heat often reaches into the nineties, with virtually no shade to moderate the sun's rays. High winds are common, and so blowing dust and sand frequently make the conditions even worse.

But as challenging as Chaco Canyon is to visit, that's where I wanted to end my pilgrimage across America. I'd hoped to make a trip there a decade ago, only to have rain ruin my plans. Now it was time to try again, because it felt right to bookend my pandemic wanderings with trips to the Land of Enchantment, as New Mexico's official nickname aptly describes the state. I'd begun my explorations at Chimayó, the shrine with the holy dirt, and would end them at one of the world's most significant archaeological sites, a spiritual destination of almost mythic status.

Exhibiting typical Chaco orneriness, even the process to reserve a campsite was aggravating. I spent more than a week clicking on an online reservation form as soon as new sites were released by the park, only to be frustrated when the sites immediately filled. I could hardly believe it one morning when my reservation finally went through.

"We're going to Chaco Canyon!" I called out to Bob. "I managed to get us two nights there!"

"I hope the car survives," Bob replied.

THE CHACO PHENOMENON

As the pandemic waned, shifting from a four-alarm fire to an endemic disease that would likely be around forever, my interior state was shifting as well. Back in Iowa, my church was gradually getting back to more-normal routines again, and my memories of the misery of Zoom worship were fading. Chaco Canyon would be a place to reflect on all I'd learned on The Road—the metaphorical one, not the one leading into the canyon—during the past two years.

Despite its remoteness, Chaco Canyon has long attracted pilgrims. Between 850 and 1250 CE, it was the center of a far-flung complex of sites linked by economic, cultural, political, and ceremonial ties. The so-called Chaco Phenomenon

influenced sixty thousand square miles of New Mexico, Colorado, Arizona, and Utah, the region known today as the Four
Corners. The people who lived in the canyon are known as the
Ancestral Puebloans or Chacoans. (The earlier term, Anasazi, is
no longer used because it is a Navajo word and contemporary
Pueblo tribes are more closely related to the original inhabitants of Chaco.)

With its extremes of climate, the canyon has never been an
easy place to live, though rain was slightly more plentiful during the years when the Chaco civilization flourished there. Its
people devised ingenious ways to adapt to the harsh climate,
including funneling the rain that came down the canyon walls
into an irrigation system in the valley. It's not known why they
chose to settle here rather than more-hospitable regions to the
north and south.

The Ancestral Puebloans were master engineers, developing
construction techniques and architectural designs that grew
more sophisticated with the passing of years. Their most distinctive practice was the building of "great houses," which were
multilevel, communal living places with hundreds of rooms,
broad public plazas, and multiple underground rooms known
as kivas. These great houses are among the largest structures
built in the Americas before the modern age. Chaco has dozens
of them, most built in a single line next to the sandstone cliffs
of one side of the canyon. More than two hundred more were
constructed in the surrounding region. Many of these great
houses include solar, lunar, and other astronomical alignments.
While there are scholarly disagreements about the particulars
of these alignments, it's clear these people had a sophisticated
knowledge of the heavens and tried to orient their built environment to the movements of the stars, moon, and sun.

The Ancestral Puebloans were skilled artisans on a smaller
scale as well, including in the creation of beautiful jewelry and
decorative objects made from raw turquoise imported from
distant mines. Other items found in the canyon include conch-
shell trumpets, carved and painted wooden flutes, ceremonial
staffs, and copper bells. The skeletal remains of macaws and

storage containers that had once held cacao show they traded as far away as Mexico. (Cacao is used to make chocolate, and the tropical birds were likely valued because of their brilliantly colored feathers.)

After three centuries, the Chaco Canyon civilization began to decline, in part because of a fifty-year drought. Its residents moved to places that included Mesa Verde, the Chuska Mountains, and other sites in the American Southwest. The great houses were left empty of living residents, their decorative plaster fading and rock walls crumbling, though they didn't disappear entirely thanks to the dry climate. They remained as sentinels in the remote valley, speaking wordlessly of a grandeur long past.

Bob and I set out for Chaco in May, winding our way over several days to the Four Corners region. As preparation for our time in the canyon, we first stopped at New Mexico's Aztec Ruins National Monument, a satellite community that was built as the Chaco capital was in its declining years. Located near the town of Farmington about fifty-five miles north of Chaco, Aztec Ruins includes the largest great house outside of Chaco Canyon and the only reconstructed great kiva in the Southwest.

Despite its name (which was given by early Spanish settlers who mistakenly attributed the ruins to the Aztecs of Mexico), the site was built around 1100 CE by people who were skilled in the distinctive Chaco architectural style. One theory is that a group of Chacoans migrated north and worked with the local population to build three great houses on the bank of the Animas River. The largest is Aztec West, a three-level structure with more than four hundred rooms. Like other great houses, it was terraced so that most of its rooms had windows and direct sunlight, with ventilator shafts that brought air into the windowless lower rooms. Its back wall, which is aligned to the movements of the sun on the winter and summer solstices, shows the Chaco fondness for coordinating buildings with the heavens.

A walking trail took Bob and me to the top floor of Aztec West, where we enjoyed panoramic views of the partially reconstructed complex that stretches over 320 acres. The sun was intense, and I could see the utility of the structure's thick walls that provided protection from summer's heat and winter's cold. After exploring some of the warren of rooms that make up the great house, we descended into the great kiva, an underground room about forty feet across that was lit by skylights that sent shafts of light to the floor. Reconstructed in 1934, the kiva is eight feet underground, with a ninety-five-ton wooden roof supported by four massive pillars. Stepping into the center of the immense room, I felt the presence of the sheltering earth all around and thought of Dunbar Cave once again. Even though the Tennessee site wasn't the most attractive of the places I'd visited on my journeys, it was curious how it seemed to connect to so much of what I was experiencing. Kivas are a kind of artificial cave, I realized, places where the upper and lower worlds come together as sacred space.

"Great kivas like this one were made of the finest materials and workmanship," a ranger explained to me. "While we don't know exactly what happened in them, they were likely used for ceremonies and group gatherings, and they have symbolic elements that relate to the stories told by the Pueblo people to this day."

One of those stories is told by the people of New Mexico's Santa Clara Pueblo. Their ancestors had once lived in the "Third World," a place of sickness, little food, and darkness. The Elders heard footsteps on the roof of their world and so planted a fir tree, which grew until it almost touched the roof of their world. They built a ladder and placed it against the tree so they could reach the top, where they poked a hole in the roof and sent Water Bird to report on this new Fourth World. When she returned, she sang to them of a world with beautiful streams, lakes, mountains, and plains filled with animals and plants. With the help of the Sacred Clowns and First Man and First Woman, the Elders led the People through the Earth's Navel into this new world, where they were greeted by the Sun and Moon, Bear and Deer, and plants and life-giving waters. As they gathered around the Earth's Navel, they divided into four groups, each with their own clans, leaders, and special bundles of gifts. Together they recited the story of their emergence, knowing they would always share this story as they journeyed in the new world.

Great kivas like this one, the story concludes, represent the First House created by the Pueblo People after they emerged from the Earth's Navel. To this day, people come here to reconnect with their origins and be spiritually nourished.

I wandered through the great kiva, musing about the ceremonies that had once taken place here and thinking that perhaps my own culture wouldn't be so disconnected from the spiritual world if we had sacred caves like this.

A CANYON WITH MANY MYSTERIES

"Bob, there's water in the bathroom!"

"Hurrah for plumbing!" Bob said, sharing in my joy.

Since we'd read online that there would be no water in the Chaco Canyon campsite, the discovery of faucets—and even flush toilets—came as a pleasant surprise. Our journey on The Road had been as jarring and difficult as we'd expected, but things were looking up now that we were at last in the park. The campground was simple but attractive, tucked against a canyon wall on one side and bordered on the other by a starkly beautiful, semi-desert landscape of grass and shrubs.

After setting up our camper we got in the car once again, enjoying the smoothness of the concrete road beneath its wheels. We passed Fajada Butte, a three-hundred-foot rock formation that stands like a guardian in the center of the valley, and then came to the park's visitor center, where a ranger greeted us as we entered. "Rough road, I know," she said with a smile, obviously used to dealing with shell-shocked arrivals. "But now that you're here, there's a lot to explore. We recommend you tour our educational exhibits and then take the nine-mile road that leads to the houses."

Though we'd gotten an overview of the Chaco Phenomenon at Aztec Ruins National Monument, the park's visitor center deepened our understanding of the mysterious culture that had flourished here a thousand years ago. Its first exhibit placed Chaco within the larger context of the contemporary Southwest, describing how many native people in the region claim a spiritual connection to the canyon. They include the Pueblo tribes of New Mexico and Arizona, the Hopi, the Zuni, and the Navajo, all of whom have their own stories and traditions relating to Chaco. Members of these tribal nations return here frequently to do sacred ceremonies, believing that their ancestors dwell among the masonry walls built a thousand years ago. They do not call them ruins because they are still living places.

Why were the great houses with many rooms built? One theory is that Chaco Canyon was a pilgrimage destination and trading center with only a small resident population. The outlying settlements provided food, construction materials, and trade goods in return for the chance to participate in Chaco ceremonies and rituals. The great houses were designed to accommodate the large numbers of pilgrims coming for these events.

The houses are the most significant achievement of the Chaco civilization, exhibiting a mastery of architectural and engineering knowledge that was unrivaled for centuries. Constructed from meticulously fitted rock walls and mud mortar, the multistoried buildings had internal supports and roofs made of wood. While the stone was locally quarried, the wood came from sources that included the Chuska Mountains, which are sixty miles away. It's estimated that more than 240,000 trees were carried by hand into the canyon, just one part of the enormous amount of labor that went into the construction of the great houses.

Chaco's elaborate road system is also mysterious. Despite having no wheeled vehicles or beasts of burden, the Ancestral

Puebloans built four hundred miles of roads that radiated out from the canyon, with the longest route headed straight north. Up to thirty feet wide and bordered by low walls, the roads were labor-intensive to build and maintain. Some had unusual features that suggest they were constructed for ceremonial or ritual use, including parallel sets of roads separated by fifty feet and roads that led straight up the sides of cliffs. The Chacoans also constructed signal stations at high points along the road system, so that fires could be lit to send messages back and forth between regions.

Eager to see these impressive sites for ourselves, Bob and I left the visitor center and set off by car to explore the valley. At first it was difficult to distinguish the sand-colored great houses from the sandstone cliffs behind them, but as we drew closer we could see a chain of structures lining the canyon floor like medieval fortresses. After we parked and entered them on foot, it was clear that while all followed the same general pattern of a terraced structure with multiple levels and hundreds of rooms, each had unique features. Chetro Ketl, for example, includes an immense elevated earthen plaza that stands twelve feet above the canyon floor, while Casa Rinconada has the largest great kiva ever found—at sixty-three feet across, it dwarfed the one we'd seen at Aztec Ruins—and an assortment of smaller structures surrounding it. Not everyone, it appears, lived in one of the great houses.

We spent the most time exploring Pueblo Bonita, the largest of the houses, a structure that was remodeled and enlarged at least seven times over three centuries. With more than six hundred rooms, thirty-two kivas, and four great kivas, it showcases the extravagance and brilliance of the Chaco builders. I wandered for some time through the site, admiring the artistry of its masonry and the expansive views of the valley floor from its top level. I remembered learning in the visitor center that more artifacts have been found in Pueblo Bonita than in any other house in the canyon, including thousands of stone beads and pieces of pottery, ceremonial staffs, stone implements, bear and mountain lion claws, and four thousand pieces of jet. A single room in Pueblo Bonito contained fifty thousand pieces of turquoise, which is more than has been found in all other archaeological sites in the Southwest combined.

As I walked, the temperature climbed and the wind intensified. The Ancestral Puebloans certainly hadn't chosen this place for its pleasant climate, I thought. Why did they settle here? Why did they build such massive structures? The stone walls were mute, no matter how many questions I asked them.

ALIGNING WITH THE HEAVENS

In the early morning hours of August 8, 1988, J. McKim Malville made one of the most significant discoveries in Southwest archaeology. A professor of astronomy at the University of Colorado-Boulder, he had come with his students to Chimney Rock National Monument in southwestern Colorado because he suspected that a Chaco-style great house near its summit was somehow connected to the culture's fascination with astronomy. After failing to find a link between Chimney Rock and the solstices or equinoxes, he had one more theory to try: perhaps it was related to the major lunar standstill that happens every 18.6 years. Sometime after midnight, he was thrilled to have his hunch confirmed as he watched the moon serenely rise between the two pinnacles at the top of the rock— an experience similar to what can be experienced during the northernmost moonrise in the Observatory Circle built by the Hopewell in Ohio.

Malville speculates that Chimney Rock, which is ninety-three miles north of Chaco Canyon, functioned as a kind of natural observatory that allowed for the precise timing of the lunar standstill. In *A Guide to Prehistoric Astronomy in the Southwest,* he compares it to England's Royal Observatory in Greenwich, the point from which time zones were originally calculated. Chimney Rock may have set the time for major cultural and ceremonial events that helped tie the far-flung Chacoan society together. "Construction of the Chimney Rock Pueblo on such an inaccessible location only makes sense if it was planned for ceremonies involving the moon," he writes, noting that tree-ring dates for structures at the top match the dates of lunar pause years.

When I was deciding which places to visit on my quest to discover the sacred in America, I remembered my visit to Chimney Rock a decade ago and my fascination with its story of ancient Chaco astronomers. I was happy to pick up another thread in that story as I wandered among the great houses in Chaco Canyon, which like Chimney Rock has many astronomical alignments in its structures. All but one of the great houses are oriented on a north-south axis, for example, and some have windows and wall alignments that mark the solstices. The road system exhibits alignments as well, especially the road that heads north out of the canyon, so straight it could have been plotted by a modern surveyor. Its best-known astronomical feature is the so-called sun dagger on Fajada Butte in the center of the canyon. In 1977 it was discovered that during a fifteen-minute period on the summer solstice, a shadow shaped like a dagger pierced the center of a spiral chiseled into a rock near its top, a phenomenon formed from light penetrating between two nearby slabs of rock. The Ancestral Puebloans, it seems, had studied the heavens very closely indeed.

Astronomy, the oldest of all the sciences, has been intertwined with religion from its very beginnings. That's not surprising, given that the sky has always been a source of wonder and danger, bringing sunshine and storms that can both bless and curse as well as the dazzling panorama of the stars at night. People who studied the movements of these heavenly bodies gained knowledge that was useful for farmers, sailors, and those who set the dates for festivals, pilgrimages, and rituals, in the process attuning human lives to the cosmos.

Researchers in the subfield of astronomy known as archaeo-astronomy try to see the heavens through the eyes of these ancient skywatchers. Writes J. McKim Malville:

> The astronomers who preceded us knew their heavens and their stars: the Ancestral Puebloan sun watchers, the court astrologers of Beijing and Babylon, the astronomer kings of Copán and Palenque, the astronomer-architects of the great temples of India and the stone circles of Great Britain. . . . Astronomers have advised emperors and generals, predicted eclipses and conjunctions of planets, devised calendars for festivals, and established dates of planting and harvesting.

In the Bible, the Wise Men who came to see the baby Jesus in Bethlehem were part of this tradition. They may well have come from Persia in modern-day Iran, a culture known for its fascination with the heavens. Closer to our own day, the domes of many churches, especially in the Orthodox and Roman Catholic traditions, are built to mimic the celestial sphere. Gazing upward into these sacred spaces, worshipers see a representation of the great dome of heaven. Perhaps these are our closest connections to the kivas of the Southwest.

At the Chaco campground, I loved sitting outside after dark, when the heat of the day had faded and the sky sparkled with more stars than I'd ever seen before. Chaco is designated as an International Dark Sky Park at the Gold Tier Level, which means you can see a dazzling array of stars with just the naked eye. It's no wonder the Chacoans were obsessed with the heavens, I thought as I gazed upward. Because of the altitude, the remoteness, and the dry air, the clarity of the stars was extraordinary. The Alaskan aurora had been spectacular, but these skies were also putting on a show high above me. I realized that part of what Chaco was teaching me was simply to raise my eyes to the heavens. So much of my travels across America had involved looking downward—to water, dirt, and stones, from caves and mounds to peering inside a volcano. Alaska and

Chaco had given me the opposite message, telling me simply to look up and be amazed.

SACRED SILENCE

"The thing I remember most is the silence," a friend told me when he learned I was going to Chaco. "The silence is louder there than any place I've ever been."

The paradox made growing sense to me the more time we spent at the park. Because of the difficulty of reaching Chaco and the lack of accommodations inside the canyon, it gets relatively few visitors. While some hardy folks do it as a day trip, as evening falls the only people in the canyon are those staying in the campground and the National Park staff, who have their own separate small residential enclave. That means there's a lot of space and sky for each person, making this a good place to think, there amid the stark grandeur of the canyon.

Chaco made me realize that the holy sites that most speak to me have silence at their core: quiet medieval chapels filled with the lingering smells of incense, mountaintop shrines where the only sound is the wind, prehistoric circles of stones standing mutely, pagan temples long deserted by worshipers. Tourists and pilgrims may pass through, but underneath them in such places is a deep stillness. Chaco has that quality more than other place I've been. In the vastness of the canyon, it seemed as if the valley was an immense kiva, all its parts symbolically linked, creating a microcosm of the universe itself. And despite the heat, the wind, and the harshness, it somehow felt like home.

On our last afternoon in Chaco, the temperature climbed to ninety-five degrees and the wind grew even stronger, blowing sand everywhere. Bob took refuge in our camper, but I was determined to make the most of my time in the canyon. I returned to the great houses on my own, exploring several that we hadn't had the chance to visit. The heat was searing, and the wind was like standing in front of a huge hair dryer set on high. I knew that my pilgrimage to Chaco was hardly the stuff of which epic journeys are made, but still, it was plenty challenging.

A lot of people would think it's stupid to be here, I thought. And why *was* I here? And why had I traveled to Tennessee and California and Nebraska and all the other places that had called to me? I thought of the words of a Pueblo woman who'd been featured in the film we'd seen at Aztec Ruins National Monument. She spoke of her people's migration from the Earth's Navel to a variety of places before they found their home. Scholars wonder why they moved from one place to another, she said, but for the Pueblo people, there is no mystery at all. The people were on a journey, and when it was time for them to leave, they moved on. Her words resonated, making me feel better about my own wanderlust. On pilgrimage, time is irrelevant. You might stay for a day, a week, or a century, but eventually the time will come to move once again.

And now it was time for me to move as well. I stood up, shaking the sand off my pants and adjusting my broad-brimmed hat. It was time to see if long-suffering Bob was surviving the heat. I drove back to camp, where I found him occupying the tiny sliver of shade on the side of the camper away from the sun.

"This place isn't nearly as scenic as other places we've been in the Southwest," he offered.

"I know," I agreed. "But you're not supposed to stay here. If it's too wonderful you'll want to remain, and that's not the point of a pilgrimage."

We made dinner, a simple meal flavored with sand. Afterward I suggested we head out to the great houses for one last visit. With classic Chaco capriciousness, the weather had moderated by the time we got to the far end of the paved road through the valley. We set out on a hiking trail that led to the great houses Kin Kletso and Casa Chiquita. As we walked, the canyon wall blocked much of the wind and the temperature grew a little cooler. Directly above us, a dozen or so ravens began wheeling and turning in great circles, almost as if they were performing for us. I remembered that these canny and intelligent birds are considered sacred by many cultures, and I wondered if they were responding in some way to our presence. The shifting light of the approaching evening brought out subtle colors in the canyon walls—soft peach, muted orange, and striations of purple. We didn't talk much, simply enjoying the feel of the air and the beauty of the landscape. It felt as if we were the only people in the entire world. And maybe we were, except for the ancestors who lived in the canyon.

On our way back to the car, I suggested we stay for the sunset from Pueblo del Arroyo, one of the largest of the great houses. We climbed to a spot on its top level that gave us a broad view of the valley and watched as the sun slowly inched its way to the horizon, reds and pinks lighting the lower half of the sky. The quiet settled deeper around us, that immense, mysterious silence of Chaco. I was suddenly glad that The Road was so awful, even though we'd have to endure it again the next morning. It was a small price to pay for having this endless expanse to ourselves.

Tomorrow we would leave Chaco Canyon, and I doubted I would return, given its remoteness and the difficulty of the journey. What I'd said to Bob about pilgrimage continued to echo in my mind. Some places you visit but shouldn't remain, because they're part of your path but not its destination. And maybe that's why we need our local churches and synagogues and mosques, the places where we put down spiritual roots. A kind of alchemy can occur there too, transformations created by ordinary human interactions, of having to put up with people who irritate you and be with them when they're dying, of meeting budgets and cleaning floors and all the other details that go into sustaining a community of faith. These things can be as important for the soul as pilgrimage, a point that inveterate travelers like myself need to remember. I would return to church, I realized, because I needed both roots and wings.

I was grateful that my travels around the country had given me a deeper understanding of those wings of pilgrimage, of setting out on the road with a wish but not a plan, the better to respond to the messages that come unbidden. Those messages may come in the form of wind or rain, the rustling of trees or the grandeur of the night sky, an animal that crosses our path or a crackling fire. I hoped the lessons I'd learned from the powers of the earth would remain with me long after memories of the pandemic had faded.

Lines from the Sufi poet Rumi came to my mind:

> God's joy moves from unmarked box to unmarked box,
> from cell to cell. As rainwater, down into flower bed.
> As roses, up from ground.
> Now it looks like a plate of rice and fish,
> now a cliff covered with vines,
> now a horse being saddled.
> It hides within these,
> till one day it cracks them open.

My own version of Rumi's musings would speak of the spirit moving from the sandhill cranes to the bison of South Dakota, flowing from the hot springs of Oregon through the red rock of Pipestone, pooling in the deepest reaches of Dunbar Cave and sparkling upward in the northern lights, bubbling in the fires of Kīlauea, rooting deep in the dirt at Chimayó and in the mounds of Ohio, growing tall with the redwoods of California and permeating the silence of Chaco. Ever changing, ever ancient, ever new. Just keep your heart open and the spirit will appear.

Acknowledgments

In writing this book I've relied on the kindness and expertise of many people. I'm grateful to Rich Warren for telling me that I had to visit the Ancient Ohio Trail (he was right), and to Marian Wingo and Andrea Billhardt for being wonderful traveling companions on any trip, including a journey to see prehistoric mounds. Brad Lepper, senior archaeologist for the Ohio History Connection's World Heritage Program, provided invaluable assistance in understanding the significance and history of the Ancient Ohio Trail. At Pipestone National Monument, park ranger Gabrielle Drapeau patiently answered my questions and worked with me on fine-tuning the text. Thanks to Adam Neblett, park ranger at Dunbar Cave State Park, for helping me realize why the cave is so precious and for a memorable tour in the dark.

I'm grateful to Jennifer Masada and Kirk Corey for their fascinating introduction to the spiritual and cultural treasures of Hawai'i. Thanks to Mary Beth for teaching me about the spirituality of stones and to Kathy and Nancy for the prairie burn and for being my kayaking mentors.

One of my great pleasures in writing this book has been reconnecting with my cousin Debbie Mettille. I'm grateful to Debbie and her husband Butch for their warm welcome to Alaska, for Debbie's family stories, and for a rekindled friendship forged under the northern lights.

In writing a book focused on natural wonders, I'm conscious of the fact that I don't describe in detail the many threats faced by our beautiful world, though they are a backdrop for much of what I have written. In focusing on the spiritual side of nature, I hope that people will deepen their love for it and work harder to protect and restore it. I'm grateful to friends who inspire me with their passionate commitment to environmental issues, especially Lindy Weilgart, Connie Mutel, Mary Swander, Karin Stein, Elisabeth Swain, and Karin Knutson Klein. Their work on climate change, underwater noise pollution, agricultural sustainability, habitat restoration, and environmental education is part of the inspiration for this book.

Thanks to my agent, Greg Daniel, for his wise counsel and work on my behalf, and to my editor, Jessica Miller Kelley. Jessica, along with the rest of the staff at Westminster John Knox Press, make publishing a book a genuine pleasure.

Of all the books I've written, this one is closest to the heart of my husband, Bob Sessions. As we've traveled around the country, I've greatly benefited from being able to see the world through his eyes. His deep love for the wonders and beauties of nature has inspired me and many others.

During the writing of this book, my son Owen met and married the wonderful Melissa, to the delight of everyone involved. I'm pleased to dedicate this book to them, a couple who give me hope for the future of the world. May you find that every step you take together is home.

Book Club Discussion Guide

1. Have you been to any of the sites Erickson visits in the book or to other sites that illustrate the themes she explores?
2. Of the elements and themes featured in each chapter—dirt, air, earthen mounds, stones, trees, caves, water, animals, lights, fire, and astronomy—which are most challenging for you to find spiritual meaning in? Which come most naturally to you?
3. Erickson comments that water is both a source of awe and potentially dangerous. Fire, too, shares this razor's edge. Does the potential of danger enhance something's spiritual power for you, or does it have the opposite effect?
4. One of the themes in the book is the idea of a multi-level world. In your life, have you wandered through an underground realm of darkness or felt the presence of a heavenly realm? If so, what did you learn?
5. Erickson writes this about the Ancestral Puebloans: "The people were on a journey, and when it was time for them to leave, they moved on. . . . On pilgrimage, time is irrelevant. You might stay for a day, a week, or a century, but eventually the time will come to move once again." What would it mean for you to view life as a journey, both physically and spiritually?
6. Erickson writes about specific places, but her overarching theme is that entrances to the holy are anywhere and everywhere. In what places have you experienced the sacred?
7. How did the COVID-19 pandemic affect your spiritual life? Do your experiences during the pandemic continue

to influence you? What spiritual changes do you think the pandemic has brought to the larger world?

8. What insights into spirituality did you gain from reading this book? Are there any practices or places you would like to experience as a result of reading this book? Why do they call to you?

Notes

8   *"Walk as if you are kissing the Earth"*: Thich Nhat Hanh, *Peace Is Every Step: The Path of Mindfulness in Everyday Life* (New York: Bantam Books, 1992), 28.

17   *"I always tell people that I have no faith"*: Erik Eckholm, "A Pastor Begs to Differ with Flock on Miracles," *New York Times*, February 20, 2008.

18   *"From then on, I was always on my way back"*: Lesley Poling-Kempes, "A Call to Place," in *Georgia O'Keeffe and New Mexico: A Sense of Place*, ed. Barbara Buhler Lynes, Lesley Poling-Kempes, and Frederick W. Turner (Princeton, NJ: Princeton University Press; Santa Fe, NM: Georgia O'Keeffe Museum, 2004), 78.

19   *"To me, [bones] are as beautiful"*: Georgia O'Keefe, quoted in "The Natural World" (past exhibition), https://www.okeeffe museum.org/installation/the-natural-world/

40   *"[Scientists have] discovered"*: James Nestor, *Breath: The New Science of a Lost Art* (New York: Riverhead Books, 2020), xix.

72   *"With this sacred pipe"*: Joseph Epes Brown, *The Sacred Pipe: Black Elk's Account of the Seven Rites of the Oglala Sioux* (Norman: University of Oklahoma Press, 1953), 5–6.

85   *"Wood once constituted the greatest part"*: William Bryant Logan, *Oak: The Frame of Civilization* (New York: W. W. Norton, 2005), 21.

93   *"This forest was like the Internet"*: Suzanne Simard, *Finding the Mother Tree: Discovering the Wisdom of the Forest* (New York: Alfred A. Knopf, 2021), 225.

93   *"There's so much more going on"*: Suzanne Simard, quoted in Diane Toomey, "Exploring How and Why Trees 'Talk' to Each Other," *Yale Environment 360*, September 1, 2016.

97   *"For at the dawn of history"*: Sir James George Frazer, *The Golden Bough: A Study in Magic and Religion* (New York: Macmillan, 1922), 126.

104 *"From the early Greek and Roman physicians"*: Wallace J. Nichols, *Blue Mind: The Surprising Science That Shows How Being Near, In, On, or Under Water Can Make You Happier, Healthier, More Connected, and Better at What You Do* (New York: Little, Brown, 2014), 155.

110 *"In the world of relative truth"*: Thich Nhat Hanh, *The Heart of the Buddha's Teaching: Transforming Suffering into Peace, Joy, and Liberation* (New York: Broadway Books, 1998), 125.

110 *"The Tao that can be told"*: Lao Tzu, *Tao Te Ching*, trans. Gia-Fu Feng and Jane English (New York: Random House, 1972), 1.

110 *"Under heaven nothing is more"*: Lao Tzu, *Tao Te Ching*, 78.

112 *"Who can wait quietly while"*: Lao Tzu, *Tao Te Ching*, 15.

118 *"The fact that for more than 20,000 years"*: Jean Clottes, "Ritual Cave Use in European Paleolithic Caves," in *Sacred Darkness: A Global Perspective on the Ritual Use of Caves*, ed. Holley Moyes (Boulder: University Press of Colorado, 2012), 25.

124 *That said, I must admit*: information on Mississippian art is from Will Hunt, "Artists of the Dark Zone," *Archaeology Magazine*, November/December 2019, https://www.archaeology.org /issues/358-1911/features/8074-america-southeast-cherokee-caves.

125 *"Caves are often mentioned"*: Beau Duke Carroll, "Talking Stone: Cherokee Syllabary Inscriptions in Dark Zone Caves," master's thesis, University of Tennessee, 2017, p. 27, https://trace.tennessee .edu/cgi/viewcontent.cgi?article=6392&context=utk_gradthes.

127 *"Where you stumble, there lies"*: *A Joseph Campbell Companion: Reflections on the Art of Living*, selected and ed. Diane K. Osbon (New York: HarperCollins, 1991), 24.

138 *"perfect storm"*: Dan Flores, "Reviewing an Iconic Story: Environmental History and the Demise of the Bison," in *Bison and People on the North American Great Plains: A Deep Environmental History*, ed. Geoff Cunfer and Bill Waiser (College Station: Texas A&M University Press, 2016), 43.

144 *"Nobody really pretends to take the augury seriously"*: Boria Sax, *The Mythical Zoo: Animals in Myth, Legend, and Literature* (New York and London: Overlook Duckworth, 2013), 219.

160 *"On the eastern horizon the darkness"*: Lucy Jago, *The Northern Lights: The True Story of the Man Who Unlocked the Secrets of the Aurora Borealis* (New York: Alfred A. Knopf, 2001), 8–9.

163 *"In order to ascend from the lowest"*: Virginia Chieffo Raguin, *The History of Stained Glass: The Art of Light, Medieval to Contemporary* (London: Thames & Hudson, 2003), 13.

167 *"I have learned things in the dark"*: Barbara Brown Taylor, *Learning to Walk in the Dark* (New York: HarperOne, 2014), 5.

171 *Beginning in the third century*: Story adapted from *Desert Fathers and Mothers: Early Christian Wisdom Sayings, Annotated and Explained*, annotation by Christine Valters Painter (Woodstock, VT: Skylight Paths, 2012), 137.

176 *"The presence of Pelehonuamea"*: "Pele," National Park Service, Hawai'i Volcanoes National Park, https://www.nps.gov/articles /pele.htm#:~:text=The%20presence%20of%20Pelehonuamea %20is,land%20and%20this%20sacred%20landscape.

177 *"Blessed are You, Eternal our God"*: "Shabbat Blessings: Upon Lighting the Candles," ReformJudaism.org, https://reformjudaism .org/beliefs-practices/prayers-blessings/shabbat-blessings-upon -lighting-candles.

177 *"Earth alone holds fire"*: Stephen J. Pyne, *The Pyrocene: How We Created an Age of Fire, and What Happens Next* (Oakland: University of California Press, 2021), 7.

177 *"The more we try to remove fire"*: Pyne, *The Pyrocene*, 3.

179 *"If the landscape reveals one certainty"*: Annie Dillard, *Pilgrim at Tinker Creek* (New York: HarperPerennial Modern Classics, 2013), 11.

196 *"Construction of the Chimney Rock pueblo"*: J. McKim Malville, *A Guide to Prehistoric Astronomy in the Southwest* (Boulder, CO: Johnson Books, 2008), 99.

197 *"The astronomers who preceded us"*: Malville, *A Guide to Prehistoric Astronomy in the Southwest*, 3–4.

201 *"God's joy moves from unmarked box"*: Jalal Al-Din Rumi, *The Essential Rumi*, trans. Coleman Barks, with John Moyne (New York: HarperCollins, 1995), 272.

About the Author

From a childhood on an Iowa farm, Lori Erickson (www.lori erickson.net) grew up to become one of America's top travel writers specializing in spiritual journeys. She is the author of *The Soul of the Family Tree: Ancestors, Stories, and the Spirits We Inherit; Near the Exit: Travels with the Not-So-Grim Reaper;* and *Holy Rover: Journeys in Search of Mystery, Miracles, and God.* Her work has appeared in the *Los Angeles Times, National Geographic Traveler, Travel + Leisure,* and *Better Homes & Gardens,* among others. Lori lives in Iowa City, Iowa, with her husband, Bob Sessions, who frequently serves as her photographer on assignments. She's the mother of two adult sons.